MINIMALIST HOMESCHOOLING

A values-based approach to maximize learning and minimize stress

A step-by-step guide to an intentional education while freeing up time, energy, and space

By Zara Fagen, PhD

This book is dedicated to my children who remind me in their small ways that life doesn't have to be stressful; and to my husband who has patiently waited for me to figure that out.

Table of Contents

Chapter 1

HOW MINIMALISM LOOKS IN HOMESCHOOLING

Make things as simple as possible but no simpler.

-Albert Einstein

Minimalism embraces a simplified life. Minimalist homeschooling embraces a simplified plan.

Minimalism advocates living only with the things that you truly love or need. Minimalist homeschooling advocates a focus on specific subjects and goals according to what the student truly loves and needs in their education.

Minimalism empowers people to save space, time, money, and energy by shunning mass consumerism and the have-it-all, do-it-all lifestyle rampant in our modern world. Minimalist homeschoolers save space, time, money, and energy by avoiding the temptation of the do-it-all (exactly like everyone else) mentality common in homeschoolers.

1

Minimalism offers freedom through the removal of the clutter in our homes. Minimalist homeschooling offers freedom by the removal of clutter in our children's education; through thoughtful planning to create an uncluttered education plan based on values and goals.

Shortly after my third child was born, I met a delightful woman who came to me for some natural wellness information. She homeschooled two children a few years older than my own and became a good friend very quickly. She was minimalist before minimalism was a thing. I was intrigued. Her space was sparse; all surfaces were cleaned. She had a strict one-thing-in-one-thing-out policy to which she actually adhered. She only wore awesome designer clothes (purchased mostly second-hand) and her home was clean. She hit the donation box almost every week, one bag at a time. Her home seemed so easy to care for. It was easy for her to have us over anytime, whereas I was always frantic for at least 24 hours prior to guests arriving, and apologizing if someone arrived unannounced. What's more, she was also very practical as a homeschooler: never overfilling her children's schedule, yet completely confident in their education. She inspired me. I wanted her Zen.

Now, five years later, I am sharing my journey from frantic homeschooling mother to calm and content homeschooler in this guide. I want others to see that homeschooling doesn't have to mean a crazy, busy life of too much to do, too much to buy, and too much to plan. There *is* a way for your children to learn more while doing less.

Minimalist homeschooling is not about taking the easy route or being lazy! Minimalist homeschooling is not squeaking by with the bare minimum, or ignoring education until it is a necessity. It is not just going through the books that have the appropriate grade number in the top right corner and checking off a list that somebody else has made. Minimalist homeschoolers invest their time and energy in the front-end of the process, carefully choosing subjects and resources to best achieve specific values and goals. It is an incredibly thoughtful and intentional approach to homeschooling.

While minimalism advocates loving everything to which you dedicate time, space, and energy, it isn't an excuse to go and buy all-new décor, just because you don't love what you have. Instead, minimalism advocates living with less. It is the opposite of consumerism. If you don't love your throw pillows anymore (or picking them up off the floor 5 times every day), then get rid of the throw pillows and live without them. If your children only use a certain kind of markers, do not buy the others because they are cheap, and do not save the others "just in case." Invest in the markers your children love and no others.

Learn to see the value in empty space. That unfilled space lowers your cortisol levels and creates a welcoming and serene atmosphere. That open space represents time diverted from dusting and organizing that can be redirected to being who you'd like to be.

Similarly, minimalist homeschooling is not about throwing out everything you have ever done. It is about assessing what you love, and what your family needs in their education and life. Minimalist homeschooling progresses along the course of greatest value, but it is not about cramming in more of the latest and greatest in search of an allusive perfect ideal. Minimalist homeschooling advocates giving your best efforts, attention, and energy to your highest priorities in order to create a less cluttered life.

Minimalist Homeschool Mindset Hack #1
Do what you love; use what you love.

If homeschooling feels hard every day – if you feel over-burdened, if you are always busy, but never sure of what you have accomplished – then I wrote this book for you. I was that person. I tried different styles, different curricula, different books, different schedules, and a different space – but really, **I needed a different**

mindset and a different approach.

If what you have tried so far hasn't worked, it is probably not because you are flawed, but rather perhaps because you were trying to do it all, instead of holding your values and goals in a place of primary importance. The simultaneous simplification and focus of minimalist homeschooling can get you on a road to a calm, stress-free, purposeful, and confident homeschool.

Life is simple, though not necessarily easy. That is what I tell myself whenever life feels overwhelming. Life is simple, not easy. Wake up each day and be who you want to be. It is simple, not easy. If life feels hard, complicated, uncertain, frustrating, or too busy, ask yourself if you are *being* who you want to *be*. Often we judge our lives (and our successes) by what (or how much) we are doing, or by what (or how much) we have. Our innermost self becomes in conflict with our outward action; we get so caught up in the doing and the having, that we forget to just BE.

Early in our marriage, my husband and I listened to an audio book together about values-based financial planning called Smart Couples Finish Rich. In the book, David Bach describes three uses for money: having what you want to have, doing what you want to do, and being who you want to be. He makes the argument that many people prioritize spending their money on *having* over *doing* and *being.* In reality, he suggests that we should be spending our money first on *being* who we want to be. You are far more likely to be satisfied with your investment in the long-term if it supports your values. To say it another way: people are happier when they invest in being who they'd like to be, instead of investing in something to have.

Long before the minimalist rally against consumerism got a name, this truth resonated with Danny and me. We knew that we wanted to "be," and "do," far more than "have." We also knew that we would have to be very deliberate and intentional with our money in order to swim against the mainstream current that preaches having the latest technology, vehicle, style, toy, or thing in order to achieve happiness and fulfillment.

Ten years later, we were homeschooling, business-owning parents of four children, still swimming against the consumer current. But instead of feeling free and purposeful, it felt difficult and exhausting. Not to take the metaphor too far, but I felt like I was drowning. No matter how hard I tried, my head was barely above water; I was treading water and making no progress.

Do you know that feeling of drowning in life? It was a huge moment when I realized that the intentionality that we had applied to our finances could also be applied to my time and energy. Think of it this way: we are happiest when we invest our *time* and *energy* in being who we'd like to be! If we were using our most important core values to dictate how we spend our money, why wasn't I using that same method for deciding how to spend my time? While hard work and actions with good intentions had gotten us far, it had completely overwhelmed me. Our lives were far from simple, much less relaxing. Here's what I learned: Hard work and good intentions, without priorities and focus are a quick way to overwhelm.

It occurred to me that rather than reinventing our schedule and our to-do's over and over and over again for the hundredth time, trying to conjure up a way to do it all, I instead needed to revisit the truth that we had discovered a decade prior: our priorities are to *be,* not to *do,* or especially not to *have.* I had let homeschooling and business turn into a never-ending to-do list of things that could or "should" be done. Instead, our time and energy needed to be dictated by a thoughtful list of core values.

Minimalist Homeschool Mindset Hack #2
Invest your time and energy in your values.

What's more, I could apply this mindset to our

homeschool. Education and knowledge, with all of the facts, workbooks, projects, lessons, books, and subjects involved, can become a new laundry list of things to have. You can hoard the supplies and knowledge with the attitude of owning it, getting it, and having it. The focus is on having – on passing to the next book, the next grade, or the next project. Instead of focusing on educational values like self-discipline, creativity, curiosity, service, and hard work, you are looking for value in the completion of tasks and the assimilation of facts.

When we focus on the doing, and the having, rather than the being in homeschooling, life starts to feel busy, frustrating, uncertain, and tedious. That is, hard. However, when I focus on being the type of mother and teacher I want to be and encourage my children to be the type of learners that I would like them to be, things are simplified. It takes conscious effort to focus, to be who you would like to be, and to encourage children to be the best version of themselves. It can be exhausting. But it doesn't feel uncertain or complicated. It is difficult to keep from screaming some days, but it is easier to calm down when the focus is on *who* we are rather than *what* we are accomplishing.

This is not to say that minimalist homeschooling doesn't value accomplishment. Instead, it is an understanding that if someone is *being* who they want to be, with goals and values in the forefront of their minds, then *doing* appropriate things automatically flows from that mindset. Furthermore, if you are *being* who you want to be, and therefore *doing* what you want to do, then *having* the appropriate skills and knowledge necessarily follows. We want to keep homeschooling simple, yet squeeze every drop of goodness from each minute we spend schooling... or living. For this reason, minimalist homeschooling starts with a foundation of personal educational values.

In order to go against the typical do-it-all mindset, minimalist homeschooling ignores what "everybody else" is doing. Minimalist homeschooling ignores "should." And while we're at it, minimalist homeschooling ignores "might."

"Everybody else" is an indication that we are looking externally for direction. Everybody else is good for suggestions, opinions, advice, and ideas. But everybody else doesn't ultimately know what is best for your family. Therefore, everybody else should not be dictating what your family does. My intention is to take away the negative self-talk associated with trying to school the way someone else does it, and comparing yourself to how they do it. I want to empower you to create your own ideal homeschool that honors who you are as a family. No excuses, no apologies. You were made to do what you do, with the talents you have to do it. You are meant to excel.

"Should" indicates an overdeveloped sense of obligation. Why "should" you? You are obligated first and foremost to God, yourself, and your family. If you "want" something for your family because it aligns with your values or goals, then say that you want it. Minimalist homeschooling is giving yourself permission to focus on what is most important. Period. You can take your focus off of what you *should* be teaching. Instead, embrace your learning in the context of your values and who you *want* your family to be: what you *want* your family to know. We are all much more motivated to act on our "wants" rather than our "shoulds." "Should" imposes someone else's values on your decisions. If your homeschool feels like a chore, reframing your mindset from *should* to *want* can put the ease and joy back into teaching and learning.

"Might" indicates a sense of uncertainty. When we are living in accordance with our values, we are no longer uncertain about the right things to do in order to be who we would like to be. When we add clarity, simplification, and focus to our days and our school, through priorities and goals, then *might* falls away from our vocabulary. Questions like *"do we need it this season?"* deserve a "yes" or "no" answer.

Many people find it daunting to pick and choose

their own resources, and question themselves if a boxed curriculum doesn't work. Even people who do tweak lesson plans and design their own curriculum struggle with self-doubt. I believe that most of this doubt is externally imposed by watching others and comparing ourselves with them. If we look internally at our core values and our goals to assess what is most important in our individual homeschool, then planning becomes both simple and confident. If you find yourself making any assessment that includes one of those three phrases – everybody else, should, or might – immediately consider what is most important to your homeschool instead. The detailed steps in this book will lead you to that clarity and confidence that you crave.

Minimalist Homeschool Mindset Hack #3
Erase "should" from your vocabulary...
and "might" and "everybody else" while you're at it.

Children are watching your example. Research shows that the best indicator of what a person will do is what their parents did. That is a heavy realization. One reason I minimally homeschool is because I want my children to grow up working with meaning. I want my children to be people who intentionally choose how they will work, with a goal and a reason in mind.

Minimalist homeschooling is not a specific curriculum or set of books. It is not even a teaching method or learning style. I am not here to advocate for a particular curriculum or set of books. I will not give you lesson plans, schedules, or learning objectives. There are people who will, but I believe that any style of learning can fit into a minimalist homeschool through conscientious planning. A one-size-fits-all approach to schooling assumes that we all share the same values, learning styles, goals, and priorities. I do not think that is likely, so I want to empower you to choose what will work best for your family. Let's work smarter, not harder, to teach our children the most important things; and you get to decide what the most important things are.

The point of this book is not to tell you what to choose, but rather *how* to choose your materials. This book is about shifting your mindset as you create lesson plans specifically designed around the goals and values of your family. The purpose of this mindset is to break free from overcrowded schedules and the do-it-all mentality that is so rampant in American society. Your homeschool journey does not have to feel hard, or busy, or exhausting.

This book will walk you through detailed steps to create your own minimalist homeschool that will suit your family's needs. We will spend time discussing values, priorities, and goals. You will spend time thinking about your family and your time. Consider it your own personal workshop for homeschool planning. Do not be like me and try to get through the whole thing in one day. Take your time. Giving yourself ample time to complete these steps will save you time later. Find support for your mission, too. We have an active facebook community (at "Minimalist Homeschooling with Zara, PhD" www.facebook.com/groups/minimalisthomeschoolingzara), and I regularly blog and send newsletters on the topic at www.ZaraPhD.com. In fact, there is an entire series of posts going deeper into the Minimalist Homeschooling Mindset on that site. Surrounding yourself with others who have a shared mission is a great way to ensure success, and we would love to meet you.

You are investing your time into your homeschool planning upfront so that it will run smoothly (and minimally). Make the investment of time now. By identifying specific values, priorities, goals, and schedules now, you will simplify your homeschool, add clarity to your lessons, and find time in your days.

Chapter 2

FINDING YOUR WHY

Ego says: "Once everything falls into place,
I will find peace."
Spirit says: "Once I find peace,
everything falls into place."

-Marianne Williamson

In order to invest time and energy into decluttering your home, life, or school, you have to see a benefit. Bowing to pressure from your mother-in-law will not make this a productive project. In this chapter, we will think about your motivation to homeschool and your motivation to do it minimally. Since minimalism is a mindset and a new way of living and thinking, it is important to make it a positive change. It is important to embrace it as a philosophy; an ideal aligned with your values. It is important to give minimalist homeschooling an accurate name that will be encouraging and sustainable. If you would like to have more free time, be less doubtful of your progress, or would like less stress, then you have great motivation. There are countless reasons to homeschool minimally. It's time to find yours.

> *What appeals to you about being minimalist?*
> a simplified life.
> *Why do you homeschool?*
> it's the best way to live out Deut -6:4-7

One day, and for many days thereafter, I woke up as the mother of four children, running two businesses alongside my husband, with a neglected website and unfulfilled aspirations for writing, traveling, and relaxing with cups of tea. I was depressed, overwhelmed, defeated, and hopeless. My house was relatively clean (because I was paying someone to clean it every week), but it was covered with piles: things for our businesses, things to be fixed, things to be addressed, things to go to another part of the house, things to be donated, things to hide from my children, things my children had played with, things that had not yet been hung on the walls, things to be folded, things to be stored, things for our fixer-upper project, things for school, things to put away, things for the garage... things, things, things.

my house!

yep   I dreaded leaving my room in the morning to be confronted by surfaces scattered with stuff. Some of it was my stuff, but most of it was not, so I resented my family as the source of the mess and stress. If only *they*

16

would clean-up after themselves, then that would solve our problems.

In the baby stages, you are inundated with all the fixtures for sleeping, playing, feeding, and diaper-changing (which really covers the four main areas of a baby's life). Then, as they grow, you can simplify the gadgets and gizmos, but toys, books, and art supplies multiply before your very eyes. As they enter teen years, the toys diminish, and you begin to see a plethora of shoes, clothes, and technology gizmos. All the while, the adults in your home may be suffering from an inability to manage papers. All of these stages are compounded when a family shares a space. And the worst part is that cleaning is a new kind of dreadful in a space with piles of things.

The same situation occurs in our homeschools. Once you compound the various ages, subjects, and interests, the whole homeschooling commitment can feel out-of-control, and overwhelming. Then, if you add in a sense of self-doubt, piles of all the things to do, and resources available to do it, accumulate – both psychologically, and physically.

Clearly, my motivation for minimizing was less stress, less time cleaning up, and a deeper sense of calm in our home. I wanted to be in control of our space and time, not defeated by it. Nonetheless, even with this strong pull to declutter, it was hard to actually get rid of things and to find the time to do it. In this chapter, we will clarify the minimalism mindset and explain specifically how it can be applied to homeschooling.

Many people who aren't naturally tidy suffer from a sort of perfectionism and/or frugality. They think things like:

- I might need this.

- I would love this or need it in the right space/time/activity.

- It was a gift.

- I don't want to start a project unless I have the time to do it all perfectly and completely.

- If I can't get the whole thing all done at once, then it just creates a bigger mess.

- I want it all fixed immediately, but the project is so big.

Now, let's talk about how this looks in homeschooling. Homeschoolers might think things like:

- My child might need this.

- I would love this resource for the right activity.

- I don't want to get rid of a perfectly good set that was donated to me.

- I don't want to start a project unless we have the time to do it all – perfectly and completely.

- If we can't get the whole thing done at one, then it is just going to leave a big mess.

- I want my child to learn everything, but there is just too much to do.

First, break it up into smaller tasks. Look at the trees, not the forest. One subject planned is one subject planned. You don't have to accomplish the whole thing at once. One corner decluttered is one corner decluttered. One chapter of Minimalist Homeschooling conquered is one step closer to a peaceful homeschool. You are accomplishing a goal, albeit a smaller goal than your perfect ideal. All those small goals achieved add up to the ultimate success with time. Even the Earth and Heavens were created one bit at a time.

But, here's the catch: You have to declutter. You cannot just organize the mess or move the mess. You have to be honest about what you truly need and love right now. This is an important point for minimalist homeschooling: it is not about reorganizing your schedule, or moving obligations around! Minimalism necessitates saying goodbye to some things that are not currently of value to us. Things that may have been of value in the past, or may be of value in the future, are not serving us now. We are living in the now.

Minimalist Homeschool Mindset Hack #4
Don't reorganize or move the mess.

Second, assume the best case scenario: you probably won't miss it. Next, imagine the worst case scenario: what if you do miss it? What if your child really does need that subject? What if your son really doesn't score well on his math test? Can they make do without it? Will it alter the course of their life? Can you add it in later? Can you catch up if/when they do need it? Chances are, not having that thing that you (may not even) miss can be easily resolved.

Minimalism adds time to your days. You can always buy stuff or add activities you miss, but you cannot buy or add more time. I can promise you this: the amount of discarded things that you honestly don't need will greatly exceed those things you miss. Therefore, the freedom you gain from decluttering will certainly outweigh any potential later regrets. Enjoy the space and time you're freeing up, confident that you can overcome any worst case scenario that does arise.

Minimalist Homeschool Mindset Hack #5
Assume the best case scenario.
Evaluate the worst case scenarios.

Third, choose a word. There is a movement to choose a word as a New Year's resolution: a word that will propel you and focus you throughout the New Year. I have found it helpful to choose a word that motivates and sustains my minimalism aspirations as well. It helps me reframe any emotional obligation to stuff into an obligation to my own values and serenity. For me, minimalism is redefining "plenty."

One day, when my son was eight years old, he suggested that we donate one can or box of food to a food pantry every time we ate a meal or snack (an idea that had been suggested during our church's faith formation session). Innocently, I replied, "I like that idea. Let's do it. What's our goal? How long should we do it? Maybe we could do that for Lent." He says: "Let's do it until we almost don't have enough to eat ourselves. We will still have enough to eat, but just until we *almost* don't have enough."

Humility sucker-punched me right in the gut. Could you imagine living so that you have enough, but you *almost* don't have enough? This is minimalism. It's an idea of plenty: You do have enough, in fact, you have plenty. You don't want for anything; you have just the right amount of everything of importance. It is a leap of faith. We want to have extra – just in case.

You don't need extra. Extra is extra time, extra money, extra space, and extra energy. You want to live in a confident world of "plenty," not a world of "more" and "extra." What if we stopped focusing on "almost not having enough," in exchange for the second half: *we will still have enough*? For any of us who have lived through financial insecurity, the idea of not having enough makes our stomachs sink. Maybe you're even feeling financially strained right now. But, to live in fear of anything – even the fear of maybe not having enough one day – is to live a restricted life. What freedom could you gain by realizing that you really do have plenty and taking on faith that you will continue to have plenty? Sometimes, having extra is an indication of our insecurity that we *might* need it someday.

Can we say the same about our homeschooling approach? Are we teaching things because our kids *might* need them someday? Do we collect old books and curriculum because we *might* not do enough? Do we struggle with minimalist homeschooling because of our own self-doubt and insecurity? *no*

If you can shift your mindset to "plenty," instead of enough, the world opens up. Ask yourself if your children might need to learn more. Ask yourself if your children have learned plenty. See the difference? "Plenty" instills confidence because it goes beyond sufficiency ("enough") towards abundance. The amazing thing is that we can do so much less, and have so much less, and it is still plenty!

What about books? Plenty.

Supplies? Plenty.

Minimalist Homeschool Mindset Hack #6
Trust.
Replace "almost not enough" with "plenty."

As I simplify, declutter, organize, and purge, the word that is in my mind is "plenty." As I plan our homeschool days and lessons, I hear the word "plenty." I don't feel any sense of deprivation when I realize that our family has more than enough and my children's education is abundant. For me, a notion of "plentiful" living is a blissful one. What is your happy place? What gives you a sense of peaceful abundance? Here are some other words that may resonate with you:

Content	Sufficient
Abundant	Enough
Appropriate	Modest
Simple	Unpretentious
Easy	Straightforward
Undemanding	Effortless
Minimal	Unfussy
Clean	Clear-cut
Uncluttered	Tidy
Well-loved	Beautiful
Sensible	Lovely
Gorgeous	Delightful
Stress-free	Smart
Charming	Pleasant
Calming	Soothing
Reduction	Lessening
Diminishing	Easing
Freeing	Lightening
Restful	Peaceful
Still	Relevant

Choose your definition of minimalism – your inspiring word. Insert that word every time you read "minimal." Keep that word with you mentally or physically as you journey toward a minimalist (plentiful) homeschool.

I keep talking about doing less, and having less, and calling it more than enough. I want to stop here for a minute to clarify that minimalist homeschooling is still about excellence. The main difference between minimalist homeschooling and typical homeschooling is that minimalist homeschooling gives the most important tasks top priority. Minimalist homeschooling does not just follow someone else's checklist; it follows our own educational priorities.

Trying to balance everything is not realistic. Everybody walks around talking about balancing their obligations. To balance things, by definition, means to give things equal weight – as derived from the weighing device called a balance. In life, however, things are not balanced – they do not inherently have equal weight! Some things will always be more important and weighted more heavily than others. Minimalist homeschooling honors priorities and is unapologetic about disregarding balance. Giving all things equal weight is a quick road to overwhelm.

Also, giving all things equal weight and trying to fit it all in does not do justice to those things that are most important to us. We show what is important with our time and attention. Giving equal attention to something of little significance belittles those items that are more significant. Our children see how we dedicate our time and attention, and they understand it. We know this by their frustration at a young age when what they perceive as an emergency does not take precedence over dinner preparations; they want what is more important to them to come first.

Similarly, if you are giving the same amount of time and attention to all subjects in your homeschool, regardless of the level of necessity or enjoyment, your children cannot easily grasp where your values lie. You may be inadvertently belittling a subject that lights your child up by insisting that busywork take equal importance. If you are not conscientious about your values and priorities, you may, even with the best of intentions, be teaching your children that the value lies in completing a task, rather than, say creativity. Minimalist homeschoolers will put what is most important first.

Minimalist Homeschool Mindset Hack #7
Balancing is the road to overwhelm.
Prioritizing is the way to clarity and confidence.

Some see "minimalist homeschooling" and think it is a way to "skate by" in educating your child by doing as little as possible. In fact, the opposite is true. Gone are the days of trying to just get everything done and checked off, and then being disappointed that the outcome was not as great as you would have liked. Gone are the days of doing everything, but doing nothing well; of giving 110%, but still feeling inadequate. Instead, your time, energy, and space are freed up to give all you can to the most worthy endeavors. As a result, you do fewer things, but you do them extremely well.

If we want to put the most important things first, then we have to identify our most important things. Remember when we talked about focusing on who we want to *be* rather than what we want to *have* or even *do* in our homeschools? Our values determine who we want to be. What do you value most for your homeschool? Who would you like your child to be? You can even think about who you would like to be as a parent-teacher. Honestly, why do you homeschool? Lifestyle? Academic pursuits? Religious convictions?

Identify your family's top 5 homeschooling values. These are not skills, or actions: they are values. For example, "math facts," or "field trips," or other things you want to do or learn are not values. Rather, values are the person you want to be. How would you want someone to talk about your son or daughter? What would you want said in a college letter of recommendation? What type of person is most successful in the world? What would give you a sense of homeschool success? What motivates you in the morning to start the day?

Some homeschooling values could be things like: self-discipline, curiosity, generosity, leadership, good communication, self-motivation, self-sufficiency, expertise, or creativity. I could go on and on, but I really want you to decide on your own. These are not easy answers, or easy to accomplish, but they should be simple. These are not necessarily the things on which you already focus: you may find some things you did not even realize that you value that have been neglecting. Write down all of your homeschool values. Then collaborate with anyone who shares the child-rearing journey with you and narrow down your list to the 5 most important values for your family.

At the end of this chapter are the worksheets I specifically created for this book to guide you through this step of the process. These worksheets are also available online at www.zaraphd.com. I purposely included the worksheets now (instead of in a separate notebook, or at the end of this book), so that you will complete them before you move ahead in this book. Identifying core educational values is the most powerful way to start refining your homeschool right away. Do not wait. Knowing what you want for your children is the ultimate

28

motivator. This is your road map. Simple. Provocative.
Life-defining.

1. I don't want to hear my kids say they hate learning or hate school. I want to teach in a way that's relevant to them; that peaks their curiosity; that challenges them and builds on their strengths. I don't want them to feel defeated or exasperated by the activities or lessons we do. The room set is needs to be free of clutter and trash. A blank canvas. It benefits my family by creating strong familial ties, a firm foundation for them to stand on when they strike out on their own. How else would I instill my values and beliefs in them if 80% of their time is with someone else?

2. My husband. My parents. My in-laws. My sister. My co-op. My friends.

3. Nothing holding me back except at this point. I'm ready to take the plunge. I'll do whatever it takes to get off this downward spiral I'm in. My weakness are perfectionism and frugality. I'm always keeping stuff in case I might need it someday.

FINDING YOUR WHY

1. Why do you want to homeschool minimally? How will it feel? How will it benefit your family?

2. Who will support and encourage this journey?

3. What is holding you back? What are you afraid of? What are your weaknesses?

1.

✓• self-discipline (self-governance, moderation

⊙ hard work (diligence; excellence)

✓ creativity (thinking critically, outside the box, problem solving)

✓ curiosity (sense of wonder, adventurous, willing to try and ask questions)

g integrity (good chracter, honesty, the same even when no one's watching)

⊙ determination (never give up)

⊙ mannerable (polite, appropriate)

⊙ respectful

✗ to love God and serve Him only

✓• responsibility

FINDING YOUR WHY

1.

Why we homeschool. Brainstorming our
family's homeschool values:

Our top 5 homeschool values are:

1) To love God; and others as themselves. This will naturally
manifest itself in manners, respect, and responsibility, as well as
self-discipline.

2) To cultivate and encourage a spirit of curiosity, that doesn't diminish
with age, and how to explore their natural sense of wonder.

3) To discover and elaborate upon their inherent gifts and aptitudes, by
teaching them how to think creatively, critically in all areas requiring
problem solving.

I will celebrte completing this step by...

having a drink (toast)

4) To instill within them the the invaluable virtue of integrity.
and all that follows it such as good character and honesty
and transperency.

5) To pass on the value of excellence, exp; as a product
of hard work, determination, diligence, and determination.
That anything worth doing is worth doing well as unto the
LORD and not to men.

Chapter 3

PRIORITIZING

Time management is an oxymoron.
Time is beyond our control and the clock keeps ticking
regardless of how we live our lives.

Priority management is the key to maximizing the time we
have.

-John C. Maxwell

It's 9:40 at night and Danny just got home with
yummy carry-out dinner. I am just getting around to
writing for the day... and eating... and relaxing with my
husband. That probably tells anybody reading this enough
about my life right now. The thing is this: If I posted that
last sentence on Facebook, I think 90% of people would
agree with it, or like it, or even one-up it. But I'm not
happy about it and I'm certainly not bragging about it. A
lot of people wear that kind of schedule and stress like a
badge of honor. I say it with a sigh of acceptance. I'm

telling myself that it is just a season in my life and that it will pass. I'm thinking about how to change this whole . scenario tomorrow and why the most important things didn't happen first today. It is not a badge of honor. It is something I want to change.

Let's get real: In a season, that was how my life looked. The above excerpt was taken straight from my journaling one night. There is a consistent theme in this book: **Just doing it all is not success**. Whoa! That's a bit shocking, right? Here we all are bustling around, trying to do it all. If we could get it all done, then we will believe we have succeeded!

But, "doing it all" is not realistic. There will always be one more thing you could do. More importantly, doing it all is not success. Success is giving your best to the most important things. If you are trying to do it all, you have set yourself up for failure. When we try to do everything, our efforts are spread thin, and there is not enough energy or time to give it all our best.

In this chapter, we discuss prioritizing your homeschool. But since your homeschool runs alongside all of your other obligations to work, family, friends, and various associations, you have to be honest about where your priorities lie, in general. The most important things deserve to be done well. We simply cannot do everything, but we can excel at the important stuff. And – wait for it – enjoying life is an important thing. When doing the worksheets associated with this chapter (you will find them included at the end of this chapter, and as downloads at www.zaraphd.com), think about what takes up your time and energy. Do these activities fall easily into categories of "more" or "less" important?

Have there been times when you really wanted to do something, but couldn't find the time? Did you rework your commitments to fit in one more thing and then suffer the consequences of over-scheduling? Or, did you kindly bow out of another less valuable commitment to make room for what you felt called to do? Herein lies the difference between balancing and prioritizing: a balancing mindset tries to do everything equally well, while a prioritizing mindset does select things excellently.

Balance is a fallacy. All things in life are not weighted equally. Even the same thing will not carry the same weight during all seasons of life. To maintain a sense of peace and fulfillment, we have to constantly evaluate where our priorities lie. We must accept that, at certain stages, some things need more time, energy, and attention. Since minimalist homeschooling advocates doing what you truly need and love, you simply cannot move forward in your homeschool (or your life) without clarifying exactly what you need and love most right now. Only then can you excel in those areas, work smarter, achieve a sense of meaningful accomplishment, and be the best version of yourself.

Minimalist Homeschool Mindset Hack #9
You simply can't do it all,
but you can do the most important things really well.

You have identified your motivation to be minimal. You have thoughtfully curated a list of your top homeschool values. That list now acts as your measure by which all other things are weighed. You can now prioritize your school – space, resources, time, and energy – based on their weight compared to your core values. You understand the error of balancing two completely unrelated tasks. Instead, your activities will each be balanced individually with your values.

Let's move on to school subjects. Let's put all of these ideals into practice. Let's start prioritizing.

Minimalist homeschooling says you do not teach every single subject because you *might* need them, or because you *should* teach them. Minimalist homeschooling focuses on what is most valuable right now. Focusing on those items that we identify as most meaningful leads us into a sense of significant accomplishment. The focus is on exactly what you need for excelling in an enjoyable and productive life. There are subjects you feel are necessary for a productive life and those that add joy to life. Maybe some of those overlap. Do not get caught thinking your child *should* study subjects beyond those you specifically decide are most effective for your child to become the best version of themselves. There is no lamenting a lack of **extra**curricular subjects, because anything that is most worthy is not "extra."

The best private school in our area gives all elementary school children a core education, along with woodworking, art, music, science, computer lab, sign language, Spanish, chess, and gym every week. I know this because I went to tour the school. I was touring the school because homeschooling with an infant had led me to doubt whether I was doing *enough*. At first, I was amazed by all the extra things my children would learn if they attended that school. I felt a twinge of inadequacy because my children weren't getting all of those special classes. Then I remembered why I was looking at schools: I was concerned that my children weren't getting enough instruction in what I felt were the most important subjects like reading, writing, and math. When I looked closely at the schedule, I realized that the children at this school spent 2 hours at most each day on core subjects. The rest of the day was spent on other activities and subjects. As impressive as the extracurricular subjects were, I wasn't looking at schools because my children had a lack of woodworking or sign language skills. I definitely did not need an entertaining place to put them. My children are often engaged in interesting activities. More importantly, at home, I was offering the equivalent of two hours on our most important subjects. Suddenly, the school looked like just a fun place to put my kids all day, every day.

Your educational values may not align exactly with mine – maybe you are lamenting a lack of woodworking and sign language skills – but I am simply pointing out how easy it is to let our educational values get clouded by the greener pastures of what other people have decided to do. When we are honest about what our family needs and values, then our decisions gain clarity, and we gain confidence.

Minimalist Homeschool Mindset Hack #10
Clarity and confidence come from
honest reflection about personal values.

Free time does not equate to a lack of learning, but rather to unstructured or child-led learning. Hopefully, minimizing your homeschool focus will create some free time for you and your children. It is helpful to expose your children to all different subjects, even those that fall outside of their current interests, in order to discover new interests. Minimalist homeschooling means that you do not do everything all at once. You do a select few things, and you do them the best that you can. And because your family will have more free time, your child can independently pursue their interests, join you as you pursue your own interests, or discover a completely new interest. Children can still spend that time creating, playing, reading, studying, learning, and exploring.

Minimalist homeschooling relegates the parent-teacher to a position of dedicated support to ensure progress in areas that are most needed and loved. Period. It is a big enough responsibility to dedicate ourselves to the core subjects. Yet, so many homeschoolers are acting as core teacher, extracurricular teacher, and entertainer. In schools, the core teacher drops children off with the "specials" teachers – they do not try to do it all. No wonder so many traditional homeschooling teachers are burnt-out and exhausted from trying to do it all.

It is remarkable how much children learn when their education is not being managed. In their free time, my children have taught themselves how to draw, followed complicated instructions, sewn their own felt stuffed animals, created countless creations in a maker space, fixed electronics, learned computer programming, played strategic games, created their own games, designed marketing materials, put together puzzles, and read countless magazines and books which have taught them about science, history, and more. Given the opportunity, children can support their own "extracurricular" activities; there is no need for their parent-teachers to micromanage their potential interests. Minimalist homeschooling teachers support their child's extracurricular activities by supplying unstructured opportunities – trips to the library, boxes of recyclable materials, friends, craft supplies, YouTube videos, or games and puzzles – and free time.

Minimalist Homeschool Mindset Hack #11
Parent-teachers dedicate themselves only to progress in the core areas of study; they do not micromanage free time or interests.

Let's get started. I've included free worksheets at the end of this chapter to keep you moving along. First, make a list of all the possible subjects to study or things to do as part of an education. I've included a list I once started with below. It's a bit intimidating, right? No wonder nobody can fit it all in!

1. Writing: Grammar, Literary Device, Mechanics

2. Spelling

3. Math: New Lessons, Drills, Games & Logic

4. Computers: Programming and Keyboarding

5. Reading/Phonics & Literature

6. Handwriting

7. Social Studies

8. Physical Education

9. Speech, Presentations

10. Geography

11. History

12. Fine Arts: Art, Poetry, Music

13. Religion

14. Science

15. Foreign Language

16. Latin/Word Roots

Personally, we are pretty traditional schoolers – we want our children to have a strong foundation in classic school subjects, while being exposed to many subjects. Therefore, our priorities will differ from an unschooler. We both may value creativity, but may manifest that value differently in our homes. An unschooler may prioritize time outside or a child's personal business. Maker spaces, field trips, and apprenticeships could be on your list. This is your school, your responsibility, your choices, and your options. Your list of subjects and activities may look totally different from mine. And, like me, your list will change with time.

The fact is you probably cannot do everything you want to do, at least not every day, and probably not even every week or quarter. And herein lies an important truth: rotating subjects is a valid approach. I don't just mean history on Monday, science on Tuesday, religion on Thursday, and foreign language on Friday (although that is a way of doing things, too). I mean that many schools will teach their second graders social studies during one semester and science during the other semester. Why? Because second graders are spending a lot more time on handwriting, phonics, and reading comprehension than older students, so there is inherently less time available for other subjects that year. The schools have prioritized those foundational subjects at the expense of science and social studies for this period of a child's life. As a homeschool parent-teacher, you are entrusted to make your own priorities as well.

In this way, minimalist homeschooling mimics life. During certain times in our days, weeks, months, and years we instinctively change our focus to the most pressing or interesting things in our lives. Other things –

relationships, hobbies, activities, and habits – fall by the wayside for periods of time and are replaced with necessary, new, or revived things. Minimalist schooling takes the same practical approach, ebbing and flowing along with life, taking its cues from interests, priorities, and change. Minimalist homeschooling, while thoughtful and organized, is incredibly adaptable.

Minimalist Homeschool Mindset Hack #12
Don't do everything at once.

It's time to pick your top 5 subjects for *right now* (at this season in your life). Obviously you think they all have value, or they wouldn't have ended up on your list. Which ones best support your homeschooling values? Which ones help develop those values in your child? Which ones are necessary for your child to reach their potential? Which ones do your child love? Which ones can't wait? Which ones are better suited to a later time or an older child? Which ones can you remove?

I really struggled with this part. I asked my husband to go through all of the steps with me, but I had a head start before he joined in. I had no idea how to narrow the list to our top 5 subjects. Luckily, he had some incredible insight and made the decision obvious. I encourage you to include the people who participate in child-rearing throughout this process. If you feel stuck or unclear at any point, those people can be the light illuminating your decisions.

Now, rank the 5 subjects into a top three, with the remaining 2 or 3 as optional. We will call the top three subjects "major subjects", and the other 2 or 3 "minor subjects". Major subjects are the subjects that your child will be exposed to every day. The minor subjects are those that will be studied as time permits or independently by the child. The major subjects give you a sense of accomplishment. The minor subjects give you a sense of abundance. All of them support your values.

Minimalist Homeschool Mindset Hack #13
Simplify to focus on what is most important.

There are a few tricks to prioritizing your homeschool areas of study. First, consider how you would fill in this sentence: "At least I... today?" Writing every day has really helped me center my life on my priorities. It has helped my self-esteem, because being able to say "at least I wrote a few pages today," removes any self-doubt about my productivity. What is the thing you want to do in your homeschooling that would keep your own self-doubt at bay? How does your "At least I...." statement sound?

At least we did writing and math today.

At least we got outside today.

At least the children designed something today.

At least we did our science experiment today.

At least I got my lesson plans done.

This exercise will give insight into what gives you peace of mind, and therefore, is a priority. If you are not going to feel great about your child's development because they practiced underwater basket-weaving today, then acknowledge that it is not meeting your educational priorities. Do not do that item first, or at all. Minimalist homeschooling demands that we do the most important things first.

Each child may have different major and minor subjects, but take into consideration that YOU are a limited resource. You may need to prioritize one child's needs during this season, and have all the children study that subject together, because there is only one you. For example, when my oldest son was preparing for the Sacraments, I wanted his religious education to be more formal. I made religious education a priority for all of my children so that we could do it together, even though it was not critically important during that season for the younger ones.

You can also consider which subjects compliment one another. If a child is weak in one area, say writing for example, you may choose to prioritize their favorite subject **and** writing. Then, find a way to write about their favorite subject. Since lesson time is designed to be short and effective, the student will be "doubling up" on their favorite subject by learning the facts behind it and writing about it at the same time.

I am a scientist by training, but the truth is that I cannot remember a single bit of elementary school science. So, if I am focused on being who we want to be (disciplined, creative) instead of having what we want to have (a science checklist), then I would decide that elementary science will be student-directed, and a minor subject. That is, I will introduce topics, and we will dive into the topics that most interest my children during our free time. I decided, during this season, that a more formal science education could come when they are ready for middle school-level curriculum – whether that is at 10 years old or 15.

As you prioritize your homeschool, consider which subjects lend themselves to child-led or independent study, and in fact, are more likely to make an educational impact in that format. Oftentimes, when I know that a child is independently reading every book that they can find on a subject – like the American Revolution – I will take that subject off of our top priority list for that season, because I know that they are getting a lot of exposure independently and enjoying meaningful learning. Or, maybe I would make it a secondary priority, so that I supplement their interest with field trips and activities as time permits. As you evaluate your priorities, carefully consider what your child learns independently, or what you would like them to explore independently.

Finally, I urge you, when you are choosing your priorities, please consider your child's strengths. Each of us is endowed with special talents. Yet, in our culture, we tend to take a standardized test (or random Facebook quiz) and obsess over improving our weaknesses, instead of focusing on maximizing our strengths. In minimalist homeschooling, children do not completely neglect a subject that does not come naturally to them; but the minimalist homeschooling mindset reveals that it is ridiculous to focus on bolstering weaknesses at the expense of nurturing natural talents.

We can accept the importance of proficiency in all subjects, while really encouraging a child to excel in their natural talents. These are the areas where your child will change the world. While every professional must be able to communicate with proper grammar and compose an

49

email, your mechanically-minded daughter is not likely to change the world with her novels and newspaper journalism. So please, resist the urge to panic about a child's weaknesses. You can take weaknesses in stride and make them a minor subject until competency is achieved. Consider making a weak subject one of your priorities if you truly feel that it is, or will, hold your child back from reaching their full potential. Meanwhile, dive right into what the child loves and understands easily – the subject your child "gets." Make it a priority to cultivate their favorite subject, for these three reasons:

1. To encourage a love of learning.

2. To maximize their potential.

3. To build confidence.

Minimalist Homeschool Mindset Hack #14
Prioritize strengths.
You are good at it for a reason.

We are not designed to be perfectly proficient at everything. How boring. We are all great at something. Everyone knows something you don't know. Minimalist homeschooling advocates working with your own strengths and talents. If your days feel hard and burdensome, it could be because you are not relying on your particular strengths. Similarly, children will feel like schooling is hard when tasks are aligned with their weaknesses more often than their strengths. Minimalist homeschooling is all about working smarter, not harder. Therefore, minimalist homeschoolers are acutely aware of their personal strengths and use them as often as possible. I have included space on the worksheets that I designed for this chapter for you to reflect on the strengths of the members of your homeschool.

If you are struggling to omit subjects because you are afraid to neglect anything, try to assume the best case scenario and evaluate the worst case scenario, as we discussed in Chapter 2. Remember that you are making the best decision that you can for your homeschool right now for **this season only.** Once you have achieved your goals, or realize that you need to redirect your efforts, you will revisit this whole process to create a homeschool plan for the next season of your family's life. You can always add, adjust, tweak, correct, and scrap anything at that point. I have added some space on the worksheet for you to make notes about next season.

By prioritizing our homeschool subjects, we are acknowledging that in life, different parts require more dedicated attention at different times. Nothing stays the same – our children's interests and proficiencies, our family's challenges, and even our academic understanding of the world change with time – but using your values as your northern star will allow everything to fall into place as seasons change.

Next, for each subject (and each child), name some goals that you would like to achieve. This will be particularly useful as we think about lesson-planning. Remember that goals should align with your values, necessities, and happiness. Your list of goals does not have to be perfect, or complete; they are intended to be a rough roadmap that can change with time.

Minimalist Homeschool Mindset Hack #15
Goals highlight what is truly necessary.

If things do not go perfectly in the first season, do not be surprised: things rarely go perfectly in real life. Continue to tweak and refine your homeschool. It is exactly for this reason that I have given you the toolbox to assess your students' needs and create an appropriate plan – one that won't keep you at your desks all day long, sacrificing time and energy. I am a perfectionist and so the pressure to perfectly choose what my children need can be paralyzing. With this system, however, I fully expect to reassess our family's needs every quarter or semester, or maybe even more frequently if we feel we're missing the mark. Once one set of goals is achieved, move on to a new set of goals, keeping any subjects as priorities that still need focus, trading out others that are less pressing now, and adding subjects in which you discover you have a renewed interest or potential neglect.

Minimalist homeschooling is a mindset. Before you stress too much about exactly how each subject will look, rest assured that future chapters will address scheduling and lesson-planning. Resist the urge to do more than identify your subjects and goals at this point. Your only task now is to prioritize the topics that are most deserving of your time and energy. Your goal is to clarify the most valuable components of your homeschool so that you can get the most out of your time educating your children.

Minimalism advocates surrounding yourself with only those things you need and love. Minimalist homeschooling is designed to ensure your time and energy are occupied first and foremost with what you need and love. Remember that my list of subjects may look totally different from yours. Minimalist homeschooling is not a style of teaching – you could insert Charlotte Mason, Classical, or unschooling methods into this program interchangeably, with a little creativity. Minimalist homeschooling is a way of simplifying your focus as a parent-teacher to ensure that, regardless of which style you choose, you are maximizing your time learning, minimizing your stress, and acting with clarity and confidence.

PRIORITIZE

What gets your time and energy right
now? Do they fall into categories of more
or less important? Which best support
who you want to be? Which don't?

Brainstorming possible subjects:

LET'S **DO IT**

Minimalist
Homeschooling

PRIORITIZE

Child: Season:

MAJOR SUBJECTS   GOALS
1.

2.

3.

MINOR SUBJECTS
4.

5.

6
.

Thoughts and notes for next season:

How will you reward yourself for
completing this section?

**Make copies of this page for each child

Chapter 4

MAKE THE TIME

Love begins at home,
and it is not in how much we do...
but how much love we put into that action.

-Saint Teresa of Calcutta

Has time been a big stumbling block on your homeschooling journey? Time is one of the biggest motivators for minimalist homeschooling – there is just so much to do! Sometimes, when we feel like we have performed inadequately as a parent or a teacher, it is actually because we have inadequately budgeted our time. Looking back through the years, so many of my negative thoughts were actually a symptom of improperly allocated time. If you have struggled with a sense of inadequacy – wondering if you are good enough because you cannot seem to do it all, or do it well – maybe your only shortcoming is how you schedule your time.

Scheduling is more than writing a to-do list; it is about being honest about time commitments: knowing how long everything actually takes, weighing commitments against values, purging your schedule, including a contingency, and taking intentional breaks. This chapter will address those scheduling shortcomings – shortcomings that can be easily addressed – so that you can grow into the teacher and the parent that you imagine. If you have been blaming yourself or resenting something because you can't get it all done, then this chapter will be powerful for you. It is time to take ownership of what is uniquely ours: our time.

My husband and I used to lead a marriage preparation ministry at our church. We met with couples planning to marry in the church and facilitated discussion on all sorts of practical topics that impact marriages – children, finances, in-laws, communication, fighting fair, addiction, and intimacy, to name a few. During these sessions with couples, we talked about how many hours there are in a week, and how all that time gets allocated, with or without a significant other. There are 168 hours in each week. Every week. For each person. No more, no less. How we choose to spend our time matters to ourselves and to all of the various people with whom we have relationships. I have carried that lesson with me and whenever life feels too busy, a quick look at how many hours are in the week, and how I have allocated that time, answers the familiar question: "Why can't I get everything done!?"

Minimalist homeschooling requires you to not only purge your space and resources but – more importantly – minimalist homeschoolers purge their cluttered schedules. If we are going to discuss priorities and schedules, we have to first be aware of how we spend our time.

Look at your typical day and record (honestly) how you spend your time – there are worksheets that were designed to go along with this chapter included at the end. If you're schooling, time your lessons and transitions. How long do you take to get ready? To prepare and eat your meals? To clean up? To get everyone moving in the same direction? To accomplish bedtime routines and sleep? Be honest.

There was a time not long ago in my homeschooling journey when life felt hard, chaotic, busy, and stressful. I couldn't do everything, much less do it all as well as I wanted. I was frustrated by the end of almost

61

every day. I suffered from all of that negative energy, simply because I had over-filled my schedule. When I sat down to analyze how we spend our time, I started with time for sleep. Sleep is a high priority. With children ranging from infant age to 9 years old, bedtimes and sleeping time spanned 12 hours of my day. 12 hours! That first discovery hit me like a ton of bricks. Granted, our older children were enjoying some of that time as free time, but I (and often my husband, too) was bustling between baths, books, and PJs (and repeat), until I scrounged up 30 minutes (hopefully) to connect with my husband before we both face-planted into bed.

With half of our 24 hours accounted for, I moved on to the next most prominent feature of our day: eating. I estimated we spend at least 3 hours on preparing meals and eating each day. We eat a lot of wholesome and home-cooked meals, and that is valuable to us, so it is time well-invested. Let's be honest, when the kids are home all day, every day, eating becomes a popular pastime. Homeschoolers do not often have the luxury of packing a lunch and forgetting about meals for 8 hours.

Getting dressed, doing basic chores, and transitions took about 2 hours. 3 hours for school (for me and the oldest; the younger ones overlapped for shorter periods). 2 hours for me to work and the kids to play. Then, just 2 hours remained, which were allocated to activities or free time for mommy. Considering the average little league game lasts 2 – 2 ½ hours, those remaining hours were quickly accounted for.

This exercise in allocating my time was sobering. Originally, I thought that we would have plenty of free time, because 3 hours of school and 2 hours of work was a consolidated amount of time. The reality is that we actually only *have* time for 3 hours of school and 2 hours of work! Any time I tried to do more, it was inevitably going to feel stressful and require us to sacrifice something else. Instead of knowing the reality of the situation, I spent too much time beating myself up, feeling guilty, or resenting someone or something that I blamed for the inefficiency. The fact is that there wasn't an inefficiency, just a fantasy. I wasn't an inadequate mother, business owner, or teacher. I wanted to do more in a day than I could. Period. Does any of this sound vaguely familiar?

While minimalists know that free space is valuable, minimalist homeschoolers know that free time is priceless. Hopefully, when you have completed this exercise and put your time into perspective, you can take a deep breath and put all of your past fears of inefficiency or inadequacy into perspective, too. Hopefully, accounting for your time will affirm the importance of making the most of your time. Simplifying your time, your school, and your space to accommodate what is most important is not optional. If you do not guard those things that are most deserving of your time, they will not get the time that they deserve. Any number of things can creep into your schedule and divert your attention. As a result, minimalist homeschoolers purge their schedules aggressively. You can always refill a space with things, but you can never recover lost time.

Willing and competent people will easily fill their schedules if they do not guard their time. Others are quick to tell you what you "should" be doing, because you are good at it, and they need help: you should work, you should teach homeschool classes, you should participate in ministries, you should organize outings, you should oversee a group – and on and on. All of those activities are worthy endeavors and you may even enjoy all of them. Any one of those activities alone would not be overwhelming. However, when all of those activities get stacked on top of one another, along with an overdeveloped sense of obligation, it is easy to lose control over your time and energy. All time commitments must be weighed against your values.

Competency and need are not good indicators of whether you should commit. There are a lot of things you could do and there are always going to be organizations looking for volunteers. However, there are only a select couple of people who are parents for your children, and you have also chosen to be their teacher. Consider your family's values and needs, because distraction and stress create a void in your family that others are unlikely to fill. You can be selective in your time commitments, not because you are self-centered, but because you have already obligated so much of your time and talents to your family.

Many homeschoolers fit their schooling around other obligations as time allows while they are homeschooling. Those families are then concerned that they are not enjoying as much educational time as they would like. Minimalist homeschoolers weigh time commitments against their obligation to their schooling and filter commitments through their values.

Minimalist Homeschool Mindset Hack #18
Guard your time for those
things that are most deserving,
or they will not get the time they deserve.

Minimalist homeschooling relies on being honest

about the time your school activities need and allocating sufficient time towards them. **If somebody else were teaching your child, it would be considered a full-time job.** If you were to take on a new full-time job, would you have to remove something from your schedule to make time? Absolutely. You would not expect to fit a full-time job in around your existing obligations as time allows. Did you purge your schedule when you began homeschooling? Did you make enough time to homeschool the way that you would like to homeschool?

Minimalist homeschoolers know that time does not magically appear. Not everyone will need the same amount of time to school their children, depending on the child's age, the curriculum, and your preferred style of teaching. Regardless of how you school, it takes time. Every single type of homeschooler does best when they are deliberate about the time allowed for their preferred teaching moments – whether that is time for discovery, life skills, or math lessons. The reality is that schooling your children takes time, even when you make the most of your time.

In addition to being honest about how we spend our time and guarding our schedules, minimalist homeschoolers also allow a contingency in their schedules. Every project manager includes a contingency budget. Usually, a contingency refers to a financial budget available just in case something does not go as planned. Homeschooling parents are project managers, and our currency is time, not money. Time is how we indicate the value of what we do. Remember, our children perceive what we value by what gets our time and attention. Like any smart project manager, many homeschoolers budget extra time in case things don't go as planned. Just like a financial contingency, any time in our budget that isn't spent is enjoyed as a surplus at the end of the project.

Minimalist homeschoolers are experts at building contingency budgets into both their short-term and long-term plans. Contingencies can look different for different people. I use a guideline of a 20-25% contingency in order to keep our days less stressful. Some examples of building in a contingency are:

- schedule 45 minutes of activities each hour;

- schedule a day off every week or two;

- schedule a week off (or to catch-up) every month;

- schedule every 4th month off;

- schedule 4 weeks to read a book you expect to complete in 3 weeks;

- schedule 40 minutes for an activity you predict will take 30 minutes;

- schedule 36 weeks to complete 27 weeks of lesson

plans;

- schedule an hour for dinner that your family usually scarfs down in 20 minutes;

- or leave 3 hours in each day unscheduled.

It is up to you to choose which contingencies work best for your family. Avoid overscheduling the rest of your day because you have a contingency! Contingencies are not an excuse to revert to overly ambitious or unrealistic scheduling habits. If there is time left over, you can enjoy it in a spontaneous way.

Minimalist Homeschool Mindset Hack #19
Build a contingency budget of time
into your schedule.

Now that you have seen how you actually spend your time each day, and have meditated on what is most important (or not), take some time to reflect on how you would like to spend your time each week. Using your actual time commitments as a guideline, complete the worksheet for this chapter to allocate all 168 hours for an ideal week. This schedule can be idealistic, but it also must be realistic – using the actual times you discovered that your family requires for activities in the previous exercise. Can you plan some contingency time as well?

Congratulations! You have evaluated your homeschool values, prioritized your subjects, and reviewed and idealized your schedule. Now we are going to think very practically about how we spend our days. It is time to create a basic schedule. The most popular form of a basic schedule is a block schedule, which works well to demonstrate how those 168 hours actually look on paper. I have provided you a basic weekly calendar page in the worksheets for this chapter at the end. Your job is to place each item from your ideal week onto the calendar. This schedule will not include specific tasks (i.e. math lesson, spelling pretest), but rather will show broad categories of activities (i.e. school, sleep). I like to use colored pencils – a different color for each task – as I move things around.

As you complete your basic weekly schedule, consider when you are at your best, when your children are at their best, and any other special circumstances. Put your most important activities on your schedule first, during the best time. Do not try to specify what you will do in each block of time. Try to include contingency time in whatever forms most appeal to you.

Since this book is dedicated to your homeschool, look more closely at the time you have devoted to education. You have now decided which days you will school and approximated how many hours are dedicated to learning each week. If you truly want your homeschool to be stress-free (or as close to it as possible), contingency time is not optional. There is a third worksheet that shows 5 sections, each divided into 3 parts. That worksheet is designed to outline your subjects for your children on specific days of the week – subjects that can fit into your available schooling time each day. It is as though you are expanding and adding more detail to your "school" block. As you work through this section, remember to fill only 75% of that learning time with planned material. Think about how your ideal lessons look: consider how much time you have for one-on-one lessons with each child, versus group time, and time that your children will work independently. You can choose what works best for your school. I always consider independent work separate from individual and group lessons, and group our time accordingly. I prefer to have a chunk of time to attend to my work or housekeeping tasks while my children work independently, rather than sprinkling their independent work throughout the day. There are many ways to create a preliminary schedule.

First, allocate a sufficient amount of time for each child's major subjects every day that you school. Do not rely on a curriculum, or a lesson plan that a stranger created as your guideline. Instead, consider your child's attention span, your goals in that subject, and what **you** believe is sufficient time to make steady progress in the subject. As a minimalist homeschooler, you are doing these subjects every day, with laser-like focus on your goals, so shorter lessons may be more impactful than they were in the past. We will talk more about lesson planning in the next chapter; now is a time for just estimating.

Add two or three minor subjects as time allows. I have seen school schedules that do this in many different ways. Consider these options, or design your own:

- Put all of your minor subjects on one day, and devote the rest of your week to major subjects.

- Put your minor subjects during independent time and major subjects during your teaching time.

- Have your minor subjects alternate every other day.

- Teach all of your group lessons together one day, and work one-on-one with your children during the rest of the week.

- If you choose to learn all subjects through experiences, you may choose to devote one day each week to each major subject and pursue minor subjects on the fourth or fifth day.

When you are done, this schedule will provide a generic to-do list for your homeschool days. There are countless ways to spread your education throughout the week, but only a few ways that best suit your family. This draft schedule will serve as a template for each school week during this season. Choose a schedule that feels right for your family, knowing that you have the flexibility to tweak this draft schedule as you continue through the minimalism process, and as life demands. With a school template that can be used each week, the bulk of your school schedule is completed, and you no longer have to negotiate your time each week. In minimalist homeschooling, repetition equates to simplification.

Minimalist Homeschool Mindset Hack #20
Repetition equals simplification.

Logistically speaking, there are many ways that you can place a weekly school schedule on a piece of paper. Some people who gravitate towards structure will put each subject at specific times on their planner – allowing a 25% contingency, of course – so that they know that reading happens at 9am, writing is at 9:20, math is at 9:40, and snack is at 10am. For example, the Charlotte Mason PNEU schools use this sort of schedule. Others have probably already discovered that trying to accomplish tasks at a specific time is a shortcut to frustration, simply because their family is in a season of unknowns. Infants and toddlers, medical appointments, nontraditional living situations, or uncontrollable interruptions are just some cases where placing lessons in specific time slots does not work well. Unfortunately, instead of realizing their unique needs, too many homeschoolers blame themselves for a lack of structure or a lack of discipline when they struggle to adhere to a timed schedule. I would argue that it is not necessarily a lack of discipline or structure, but rather the result of using the wrong tool for the project.

I know this situation well: I am one of those mothers who would create a gorgeous plan that took naps, and meals, and snacks all into consideration. Then the baby fought their nap and we didn't get the two things done before snack that I had planned to do. It was 10am and I was already stressed and "failing." Or, I was up all night with a child and slept-in past our normal time to start the day and spent the whole day trying to catch up. I dreaded being a drill-sergeant. I had to adjust my expectations; and expecting that I could reliably predict how any hour of any day would go was unrealistic.

I eventually learned to use a to-do list style schedule with no times on it, and instead, it is separated into similar task groups. My weekly school schedule doesn't show naps, snacks or meals, because I know that we will have to stop for those when the time is right. Since I allocated our time in the week on my block schedule (including time for meals and contingencies, and acknowledging our time commitments), I don't have to worry about having an overly ambitious to-do list. I know exactly how much time I have each day for schooling. My children know that we do the most important things first. So, they know that their morning routine will be followed by exercise and then formal learning time. Household responsibilities are completed before free time. There will be quiet time after lunch every day for the whole family. Any time there is a break, we start up again with the category where we left off. For example, if we haven't finished our lessons when we break for lunch, then we will eat and have quiet time, and then finish our lessons after our break. After lessons are finished, we will work together on chores. Therefore you will notice that, in my example below, I don't give times for specific subjects. It is up to you to decide whether you would like to use a timed style or a to-do list style for your school schedule. It is important that you choose whatever comes most naturally to you and your family. The less you have to fight your natural tendencies, the easier your schedule will be to implement.

Here's an example of a basic school schedule: reading, writing and math are your major subjects, and spelling and handwriting are your minor subjects. Let's also say that you can school 4 days each week, you have 3 hours for schooling, and 3 children. You realize that the subjects you have chosen do not lend themselves to joint lessons for all of your children, who are at different levels. Considering a contingency, you have decided to devote 45 minutes per child independently, for 3 children on each school day. You believe that 15 minutes concentrated on each subject will be plenty. Therefore, each day, your child will work on one thing independently: On Day 1 they will do handwriting independently, on Day 2 they will read to themselves and orally narrate, on Day 3 they will freewrite independently, and on Day 4 they will do math drills independently. In this case, your preliminary schedule will look like this:

Day 1: Reading, writing, math, handwriting (ind)

Day 2: Reading (ind), writing, math, spelling

Day 3: Reading, writing (ind), math, handwriting

Day 4: Reading, writing, math (ind), spelling

Alternately, for that same child, you could formally teach lessons only 3 days, and have the fourth day consist entirely of independent work:

Day 1: Reading, writing, math

Day 2: writing, math, spelling

Day 3: reading, math, handwriting

Day 4: independently do handwriting, reading, writing, and math. Add spelling.

I have provided a worksheet specifically for this chapter for making a preliminary weekly schedule. It has five compartments to be labelled with the days. Each compartment is separated into 3 sections that can represent each child, specific time slots, or individual lessons/independent work/group time. It is up to you to choose categories that suit your family dynamics. For redesigned worksheets and video tutorials, check out my other resources at:
https://resources.zaraphd.com/minimalist-homeschooling.

Look at that! You have just given your child a valuable education in 45 minutes. You allowed an hour, so nothing feels rushed or stressful. You are confident that the subjects you've included will make the largest educational impact. I love to hear all the wonderful ways that minimalist homeschoolers use their new free time: maker spaces, trips, books, in-depth expertise, nature study, art, hobbies, businesses, service projects, and life skills. Major subjects offer a sense of accomplishment, minor subjects offer a sense of abundance, and unscheduled time offers a sense of freedom to pursue interests and learn independently.

You may have more time available for schooling. Your children may be older. I do not expect that everyone can homeschool every child in an hour – it will depend on your educational values and goals for your children and how you allocate your time. Nor am I suggesting that your education stops with 3 major subjects. Rather, those three major subjects are serving as a meaningful and well-executed educational foundation.

Remember that the minimalist homeschooling mindset focuses on *being*, so that the *doing* and *having* naturally follow in accordance with our values. As a result, minimalist homeschoolers learn many things outside of their 3 major subjects because they spend their time *being* who they want to be as parents, teachers, students, and children all day long. Minimalist homeschoolers can allocate relatively short periods of time for each subject because they have embraced a laser-like focus on their priorities and goals. Major subjects, and allocating sufficient time for them, offers a framework for your education. Remember, these are the topics you decided are most important in your schooling. Minimalist homeschooling ensures that the most important things get done each day.

The beauty of using this approach, is that minimalist homeschoolers create much more free time in their schedules for additional tasks, activities, and education. Most homeschoolers have a bucket list of things that they have been meaning to do, for which they have never found the time. Minimalist homeschoolers are able to discern whether those items have not been done because they actually aren't high-value. The truth is, if you are using a focused minimalist homeschooling approach, you do have plenty of time to do other valuable things.

In minimalist homeschooling, there is no multitasking. Multitasking is a way to be distracted during an activity. Studies have actually shown that you will accomplish more, with better quality results, if you address one task at a time. Similarly, both the parent-teacher, and our children, are working smarter when they focus on one thing at a time. Therefore, your whole homeschool will benefit if you and your children focus on individual tasks.

As the parent-teacher, do not try to do the dishes while you tutor math: schedule family chore time separately from family learning time. Remember that your children are learning what you value by watching what gets your time and attention. Make every effort to show that you value education, and you value them – even more than you value clean dishes! This is another reason why minimalist homeschoolers can allocate relatively short periods of time for each subject: because they are singularly focused on that one subject with minimal pauses and distractions (I know that there will still be babies climbing up bookshelves and other unavoidable diversions, but it is our job to minimize distractions, not add to them).

Minimalist Homeschool Mindset Hack #22
Do not multitask.

As we look at our schedules, let's talk about how to take a break as a minimalist homeschooler. Minimalism is about being intentional with your time, energy and space, and breaks are no exception. Everyone needs a break and relaxation. There are two types of breaks: the everyday moments of relaxation; and the large chunks of days or weeks when you totally change your everyday schedule.

Everyday moments of relaxation are those relatively quick respites that occur every day when we take a deep breath and reset ourselves emotionally, mentally, and physically. Daily breaks can take many forms including: meditating, reading, drinking a cup of tea, making a phone call, listening to music, stretching, walking, praying, or taking a bath. Really, the ways in which one can reset oneself in 5-15 minutes are countless. These everyday moments to relax are significantly different from those big chunks of time set aside for vacations, but in many ways, they are more important.

So, you have been super-diligent about homeschooling every day. You are making progress in all of the most important subjects and you have managed to stay on task with what is most important on most days. You have managed to get everyone fed, clothed, and clean for more days in a row than you can count. And guess what? It took 110% of your energy every day. You are tired. Exhausted, even. Your motivation is dwindling. You find yourself escaping to mindless activities like web-surfing, Facebook, phone calls, circles around the house picking up random items, Candy Crush, binge-watching Hulu, or any other number of things that are not mentally or physically challenging. Then, you realize how much time you have "wasted" on these mindless activities. You notice that your schedule is falling off-task more and more

often. You are still tired. You are even less motivated.
And now, on top of it all, you feel guilty about wasting
your time. The fact is, you need down time. But, if you
are not deliberate about your relaxation, it will be a waste
of time.

Sometimes homeschoolers say they are taking a
break, but they are actually taking what I call an
"educational break." Your children see a break, but since
you will be at the beach, you have packed art supplies,
and a couple of fiction and non-fiction beach-related read-
alouds. You collect shells and curiosities off the beach and
look up what they are. The public library has an event
with a guest speaker teaching about local animal species.
Your husband takes the kids to the nearby children's
museum one day. Your kids try out their remote
controlled submarine and boat in the pool, racing, talking
about drag, and trying to adjust their watercraft to be
speedier. You go as a family to Clearwater Marine
Aquarium, home of the famous dolphin Winter, and other
rescued sea creatures. When you get home, the kids write
what they remember and probably do an ocean craft about
the different ocean depths. There's a great video about
the Mariana Trench. Newsflash: this break was not
actually a break. It was a change of venue and style.

There are real breaks. These are the times when
you make no specific school plans. Personally, as a

homeschooling mother, I have found that these are rare and hard to come by because we see the learning opportunities everywhere and we want to elaborate on them. I have to force intentional, plan-nothing breaks. It is worth forcing intentional breaks because they improve a person's outlook, energy levels, and mood, thereby making people more effective and productive.

Everybody needs some down-time every day and larger periods of down-time in every season. For those of you who are reading this, and thinking it is extreme and that it does not apply to you, I am here to tell you that it *does* apply to you. Perhaps you are already good at deliberately relaxing and you just haven't realized that you give yourself permission, and time, and space to relax. That is awesome. Good job, and keep it up. But, perhaps you imagine that you *should* be content in all of your roles so that all of life is blissful and no relaxation is required. In this case, you feel especially guilty for wanting to escape the life that you *should* be so thankful for. Breaks are actually about making the time, energy, and space for *more* gratitude, and more meaningful time each day.

Some time ago, somebody started glorifying mothers who burn the candle at both ends. It has to stop. Don't get me wrong, I am not advocating for self-centered mothering (which is a complete oxymoron). There will absolutely be times when the needs of those in your family, your business, or your home will supersede your own needs – probably on a daily basis. But being super-mom means setting a good example of what a healthy and content life looks like. Would you want your daughter to grow up to believe that her value lies in how much of her health she sacrifices for others? Then why is that an appropriate mindset for you? Why would it be admirable to sacrifice your sleep, your exercise, your rest, or your meals in order to complete tasks? Rest is a priority so that you stay healthy; and, it is a priority so that you can act with positive energy, ease, efficiency, and quality. Accept it – rest is required, and it is a priority.

Teachers in elementary schools send their classes off to other parts of the building at least once each day for lunch and recess. The teachers sit in a quiet room and eat, meet with other teachers, complete tasks in peace, and make assessments. Sometimes, they do it more than once, while the students have music, gym, computer lab, art, science, or foreign language lessons. One school that I toured drove this point home: Students were with their home room teacher just 2-3 hours each day. The rest of the day was allocated to other rooms for enrichment classes, lunch, and 2 recesses. In older grades, teachers are given a "planning period." This is not because a traditional teacher is lazy, but because down time is practical and necessary. If teachers were not given those interludes each day to breathe, prepare, and take care of their tasks, their teaching would suffer. So, if you don't want to say that you're relaxing, consider setting aside your own "planning period." Every day. In fact, breaks are required in every profession by law.

You need some time when you can be "on call" but not "on duty" every day. Being on call has a different energy requirement than being on duty, and allows you to do another task while your children are doing an activity without you. Only you know what your family dynamics are. Maybe you cannot have a planning period or be on call until your husband gets home, or until the kids are in bed. Perhaps you could task older children with overseeing lunch and recess while you tend to tasks or enjoy some quiet. Many homeschooling mothers with infants and toddlers feel that they must school during all naps, when really, the time might be more effectively spent as a break, recharging your batteries to ensure a pleasant evening. Wake up early, trade with a friend, hire the teenager down the street, ask your husband, coordinate with drop-off activities, put on a movie, wear your headphones, let them play freely – whatever it takes. Be creative and make a break happen.

Your goal is to have a homeschool that flourishes. It is difficult to have any project flourish when the leader is depleted and distracted. Neglecting breaks is another way that homeschoolers set themselves up for failure. Exhaustion is a choice: It means that you are placing more value on any number of other things rather than on your own physical and mental health. Since minimalist homeschooling is about teaching in accordance with our values, look at your homeschooling values. How many of them would benefit from an energized, de-stressed, and prepared teacher? All of them? Exactly. If we are striving for excellence – for giving everything our best – then *we* have to be at our best.

Minimalist Homeschool Mindset Hack #23
Take intentional breaks.

Be specific about how a break will look. Make a list of a few things that will truly refresh you in 15 minutes – the worksheet to walk you through this is at the end of the chapter. Make another list of things you could do if you had a couple hours. Finally, make a list of what you would do if you had – gasp! – a whole day to refuel. The best criteria for rest-time activities are:

- Something you would look forward to.

- Something that puts a spring in your step.

- Something that would bring you a sense of peace

or contentment.

Another item I want to advocate including in your schedule is dating. Going back to my time with my husband leading marriage preparation ministry, the most important message we wanted couples to take away was that it was their responsibility to protect their marriage and keep it primary. We live in a world where it's almost "uncool" to honor our relationships. We are surrounded by images of men complaining about their ball-and-chain wives and women complaining about lazy husbands. We have to take responsibility for respecting our marriage and supporting it. Only you are going to protect your marriage and make it your first priority. Don't get me wrong, I hope you surround yourself with friends who honor and respect marriage, but ultimately, they don't know what your marriage needs like you do.

When you homeschool, it can feel like you and your spouse have become business partners in the business of educating children. At worst, it feels like one of you has taken on a new full-time job with overtime and no pay increase, and time for marital bliss has been shoved aside. While I agree that homeschooling is an important priority, and is to be taken seriously, your homeschool benefits from a strong marriage. I do not know what your marriage needs, but I do know that every marriage needs connection. So keep dating, keep dating, keep dating. As you look critically at how you spend your time, do not forget to include that oh-so important time with your spouse. Dates don't have to be elaborate, but they do require time.

If you are on this journey solo, remember that intimacy takes many forms. Consider including time to connect with a best friend, a relative, or a significant other – someone with whom you can relax, share your dreams and your fears, and gain valuable recharging time.

As a homeschooler, your schedule is an important tool. If you have ever spent your days wondering why you worked so hard, yet got nothing done, it could be because your schedule was unrealistic, unfocused, or even nonexistent. Chaotic, cluttered, and stressful days seem to be the norm among many homeschoolers. Now you are prepared to make your time work for you. Guarding time for your priorities, purging your schedule, allocating sufficient time, building in contingency time, avoiding multitasking, and taking quality breaks will make your time more relaxed and productive. Waking up each day knowing that your time will be meaningfully allocated and tasks can be realistically accomplished offers a sense of peace that many homeschoolers desperately want.

Time does not magically appear; minimalist homeschoolers make time for what is most important with thoughtful planning. What's more, they do not recreate their schedule every day or week, but rather use the magic of repetition to simplify their days. Minimalist homeschoolers use a decluttered schedule that highlights what they love most to create a simplified homeschool life.

MAKE THE TIME

Track your time on a typical day. The total
must be 24 hours!

Sleeping:
Personal Care (showering, grooming, etc):
Meal Preparation and Eating:
Working:
Schooling:
Exercising:
Family Time:
Personal Time:
Other:
Other:
TOTAL:

Looking at your use of time, what surprises
you? Do you have more or less time for
schooling than you previously thought?

MAKE THE TIME

Now, ideally and realistically, how much time would you like to spend in an average WEEK on each activity? How much of that would be weekdays or weekends? Allocate your time to the most important items first. Your total must be 168 hours OR LESS!

	weekdays	weekends
Sleeping:		
Personal Care:		
Meal Prep & Eating:		
Working		
Schooling:		
Exercising:		
Family Time:		
Personal Time:		
Other:		
Other:		
Other:		
TOTAL:		

LET'S **DO IT**

MAKE THE TIME

Which time commitments would you like to
reduce? What is not getting enough time?

List three actions you can take
immediately to make your time align better
with your priorities?
1.

2.

3.

How will you celebrate completing this
step AND taking action on all three items?
This is HUGE!

LET'S DO IT

MAKE THE TIME

Put your activities for your ideal week on the block schedule
below (label each block with a 2-4hr time slot):

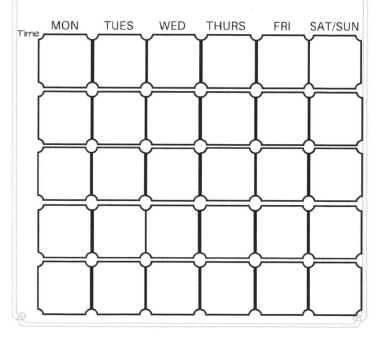

Time | MON | TUES | WED | THURS | FRI | SAT/SUN

MAKE THE TIME

Plan your school week: Elaborate on what
you will do during each schooling block
Label with children's names, days & times as
needed.

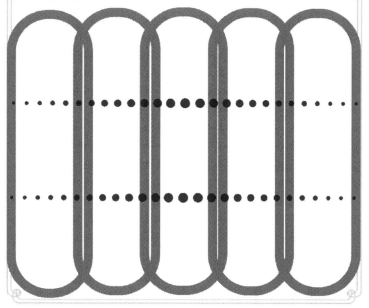

MAKE THE TIME

What are some ways that you can make an intentional break happen each day?

Brainstorm ideas for the best ways to spend 15 minute breaks:

Brainstorm ideas for breaks of an hour or more:

Brainstorm ideas for an entire day of relaxation:

Chapter 5

RESOURCES & LESSONS

Besides the noble art of getting things done, there is the noble art of leaving things undone. The wisdom of life consists in the elimination of non-essentials.

-Lin Yutang, 1895

Once you have decided on your core subjects and have your days scheduled, homeschooling is exciting again – your purpose has been established! It is tempting to immediately go start shopping for curriculum, but now is the time to minimize how you teach for maximum effectiveness. Resist the urge to purchase any curriculum (or even browse) until you have completed this chapter.

Minimalist Homeschool Mindset Hack #24
Minimize how you teach for maximum effectiveness.

Minimalist homeschooling is not a specific curriculum, but rather, can be applied to any style of education. If I were to spell-out specific curriculum choices for you, they may not align with your family's values or priorities during this season, and so I would just be offering one more curriculum choice, albeit a simple one. Instead of giving you another curriculum option, my hope is that you can take whatever curriculum you choose and apply a new *approach* to homeschooling. Once you have identified your family's priorities and time availability, you can choose the portions of any curriculum that suits your family and creates a minimalist homeschool.

Minimalism is not synonymous with being basic. There are resources out there that will outline the most standard or least elaborate curricula for each grade and call it minimal because it is basic. Those folks offer a wonderful service outlining lesson plans according to their version of minimalism and sharing them with you. However, since minimalist homeschooling is all about making room and time for those things that are of highest value to us, basic may not do it justice. Plus, not everyone has the same perception of "basic."

This book is not that. I will not lay out daily tasks or even weekly tasks for you. I will not suggest how many pages to read, how often to school, or tell you how long it will take. Instead, I am walking you through the process behind making your own homeschool minimalist. Your teaching style, your children's learning style, your desired lifestyle, your personal commitments and, most importantly, your values, all contribute to creating the highest quality learning experience for your family. Working in alignment with who you are, and who you would like to be, makes the homeschooling process infinitely easier, more effective, and more enjoyable.

My personal experience is that when a family tries out someone else's plans, they may work for some time, but then the family, for any number of reasons, falls off the wagon. They may ditch the curriculum all together, or trudge along to complete the year, or tweak it to make it work. Maybe the tweaking continues until the original curriculum is hardly recognizable. Life feels hard. Maybe nobody is enjoying the process anymore. Maybe you are wondering why you even started this journey. During all of this there is a negative little voice wondering:

Why doesn't this work for me when everyone else can do it?

I'm just not disciplined (or creative, or whatever) enough to do this.

I have babies alongside my big kids! It's impossible!

My child's learning disabilities make everything twice as long – we're constantly behind!

When you apply somebody else's creation to your unique life, it can feel like trying to fit a square peg into a round hole. One size fits all curricula, no matter how minimal, never seems to be exactly what my family needs; and based on the rampant Facebook posts of parents eagerly searching for that elusive perfect curriculum, I know I am not alone. Prepared curricula seem to have a few standard drawbacks: a subject that you prioritize isn't covered sufficiently, the lessons are presented in a manner that you don't enjoy, or the time commitment is unrealistic. Plans are biased by the values, priorities, lifestyle, and chosen learning environment of the person who designed it.

It is time to take a play from my toddler's book. He never tried to put the correct peg into the correct hole. To him, that was silly, and although he was capable of doing it, he was unmotivated to play that game. Instead, he preferred to open the container and fill it with the toys he liked best. What about you? Are you trying so hard to follow all the rules that the game isn't any fun? Could you just open your homeschooling container and put in your favorite items instead?

If you have found a curriculum that matches your family, maybe with a few tweaks, that is awesome: stick with it! Chances are, if you are reading this book, you are searching for ways to simplify your homeschool, add to its value, or increase its joy. Minimalistic living can be applied to simplify any home for any family. Similarly, the beauty of minimalist homeschooling is that its principles can be applied to any curriculum to simplify any homeschool. Working through this book, and adopting a minimalist homeschool mindset can turn any curriculum into a simple, high-value experience.

As previously mentioned, there is no educational style that is inherently more minimalist than the others. Some people may reason that a classical education is minimalist because it cycles through the information every three years, only teaching the material at an age-appropriate level, and diving deeper into topics as the education progresses. Some may reason that a Charlotte Mason style homeschool is minimalist because it relies on spreading a feast of only things that spark awe and joy, and diving further into topics that inspire the students. Some may reason that unit studies are minimalist because you explore only one topic, but you are drawing from multiple subjects as you learn about that topic. Some would reason that unschooling is minimalist, because it is almost entirely student-led learning, requiring the least planning for the teacher and using life as its own lesson. Some may reason that the three R's – Reading, wRiting, and aRithmetic – are minimalist, because they are basic.

Minimalist homeschooling is a lifestyle and a

mindset that supersedes any specific resource, lesson, or educational philosophy. In my opinion, all of those styles of learning have more to do with your personal educational values and priorities. Minimalist homeschooling is about *how* you school, not *what* you teach, or *what* you use. Minimalist homeschooling can simplify and focus any form of education. In fact, you may find that one style of teaching, one curriculum, or one set of books works best to meet your goals in one subject. Then, you may decide that another style of teaching or a different set of resources are more appropriate for a different subject, and the goals you have for your family in that area of their education. All of the teaching styles listed above can be minimalist if minimalist homeschooling principles are applied. Conversely, none of those educational paradigms are minimalist if the family is on a quest to indiscriminately check off a list at the expense of their time, energy, space, and enjoyment.

Minimalist Homeschool Mindset Hack #25
Minimalist homeschooling is about *how* you school,
not *what* you teach, or *what* you use.

Minimalist homeschooling relies heavily on personal educational goals. Minimalist homeschooling also accepts that any action is easier and more effective if it is alignment with *who you are.* Swimming against your own current is one way that homeschoolers set themselves up for an exhausting and difficult experience. Minimalist homeschoolers have learned that their homeschool feels more motivating and simple when their school is closely aligned with what comes naturally to their family, and with what is most important to their family. This is a good time to do some brainstorming about how your children learn best and how you teach best. Let's do some self-reflection and meditate on each of your children. There is a worksheet for this chapter where you can write down your thoughts. This process will help you to choose resources that resonate with your family.

For your self-reflection:

- What do you love teaching?

- How do you love teaching?

- What do you dislike teaching?

- How do you dislike teaching?

- How much time can you spend teaching without getting grumpy in a day? In a week? In a month? In a school year?

- What motivates or inspires you?

- What relaxes you?

- What stresses you out?

- What do you most want your child(ren) to gain from their education?

- What makes teaching more difficult?

- What are the best ways to refuel yourself?

- What support do you have?

- What do you need?

- What are your strengths?

- What are your weaknesses?

For each of your children:

- What is their best learning style?

- What do they like learning?

- How do they like learning?

- What are their strengths?

- What are their weaknesses?

- Is there a profession that they are motivated to pursue? Any other goals?

- What do they love?

- How much time can they spend focusing without getting distracted or grumpy in a day? In a week? In a month? In a year?

- What do they dislike learning?

- How do they dislike learning?

- What motivates or inspires them?

- What are they reluctant about?

- What makes learning more difficult? Distractions? Low blood sugar? Time of day?

Minimalist Homeschool Mindset Hack #26
Know yourself. Know your family.

Now that you have chosen your subjects and specified your goals in each subject for this season, and you have made note of what you know about yourself and your children, it is time to think about the best way to accomplish those goals. This is where your style of schooling comes in. Do you want to teach science mostly through a textbook, videos, experiments, field trips, or a combination of these? Do you want to learn history through historical fiction read alouds, memory work, or movies? Does your preschooler learn letter sounds by playing games with you, or by pointing out letters as you read together? Will your high school student learn effective communication best through a speech club or a curriculum? This is where you make your homeschool specifically *yours.* You know your time availability and teaching preferences, so be aware of what kind of learning suits your family this season, and let that dictate your curriculum choices. At this stage in the planning, be realistic, not idealistic.

I love the idea of field trips to learn and my children love them even more. But, as I neared the end of my 4th pregnancy, and my energy levels dipped to negative numbers, it was not realistic to take the older three on full-day trips. Similarly, after the baby was born, field trips with all 4 were daunting until the baby was close to 18 months old. As a result, our homeschool had few field trips for a couple of years. My husband would take the children to museums as his schedule allowed and that was sufficient. Instead, during this time, we read a lot of books and watched some really great videos. It was not my ideal permanent situation for our homeschool, but it was ideal for that season, and we still met our goals.

It is important at this step in your homeschool planning not to derail all of your previous thoughtful planning by loading up your schedule with an overly ambitious list of schooling resources. I am not suggesting that you abandon all resources – relying only on a dry erase board and a blank notebook – but rather, that you use only what is necessary and what is best. We are homeschooling minimally, so our resources consist of only what we need in order to accomplish our goals in the best way possible.

Minimalist Homeschool Mindset Hack #27
Use only what is necessary
and what is best.

In the last two chapters, you decided on your subjects and identified your available time. You have also identified your goals and spent time meditating on your family's learning and teaching styles. It is important to choose curriculum that supports your goals, that can be reasonably accomplished in the time available, and that suits your family's learning and teaching styles. Being honest about these factors means that the curriculum you choose will be easier to use and you will be more likely to stick with it. Teaching subjects that align with your educational values will automatically offer a sense of motivation. Having specific and tangible goals in each subject will create a sense of momentum as you work through them. Students who have been given a meaningful goal, a tangible accomplishment that is aligned with their efforts, or an enjoyable task, are much more attentive to their work.

A student's quality of work will clearly reflect if they are merely plodding along through meaningless tasks. Progressing through an education by achieving thoughtful and meaningful goals is much more inspiring than finishing each workbook or textbook in a sequence – for both you the teacher, and especially, our students.

Many of us have been indoctrinated to believe that completion is equivalent to accomplishment. In reality, completion is only as meaningful as what was actually achieved. You can complete a lot and see no considerable change as a result. Is completion without significant improvement, challenge, growth, or meaning really an achievement?

Minimalist homeschooling chooses resources based on specific goals. Minimalist homeschoolers don't do everything – every workbook, every lesson, or even every page in a workbook. It is tempting to try to do everything. Many homeschoolers, who find themselves busy but never happy with the quality of their homeschool, have confused completion with achievement. Minimalist homeschooling – which relies on simplifying to increase the value of the time spent educating – holds that completion is not sufficient if it is not meaningful. Rather, minimalist homeschoolers value achievement of meaningful goals over completion. As a result, there is no pressure to complete anything in minimalist homeschooling. In fact, minimalist homeschoolers will stop what they are doing and abandon it all together if it is not benefiting their goals, or if their goals have been met.

Minimalist Homeschool Mindset Hack #28
Stop doing it.
Completion does not equal achievement.

In order to minimalist homeschool, be clear about your specific goal and work deliberately toward achieving it. Some examples of specific goals are:

- Master a specific set of facts.

- Read and comprehend a specific book.

- Practice specific skills.

- Master a specific skill.

- Focus for a specific amount of time.

- Develop an awareness (for example, of other times or cultures).

- Think critically.

- Explore.

- Create.

- Communicate effectively.

- Develop self-confidence.

- Improve a specific test score.

- Discover a new interest.

Many homeschoolers will stock their shelves with every viable resource within their budget, thinking that their children can immerse themselves in the subject through these books, games, crafts, and materials. However, it is not realistic to do all of these things for one subject, much less all of the major subjects. As a result, a plethora of resources sets homeschooling teachers up for a sense of failure. In addition, a mountain of resources sets many homeschooling students up for a sense of overwhelm and uncertainty. The student and teacher are left floundering in a sea of beautiful resources, unsure of the exact purpose or goal for all of these activities and books. Finally, time and space has been filled with books, videos, and activities that may or may not encourage specific values or goals. Minimalist homeschooling is a way to create more value in learning with less time and space. Filling up our shelves with countless resources accomplishes the opposite – it uses more time and space while leaving us with a sense of being busy, but not necessarily successful.

Minimalist homeschoolers simplify their resources by thoughtfully refining what is necessary in order to accomplish their goals. Choosing only the best resources for each subject maximizes the value of the education; less valuable materials are not allowed to dilute the richness of an intentional education. As a result, minimalist homeschoolers free up the most precious learning resources: time and energy.

Minimalist Homeschool Mindset Hack #29
Do not let less valuable resources dilute
the richness of an intentional education.

Early in my homeschooling career, I was talking with a friend who was farther along in the journey. I was lamenting how hard it was to accomplish everything. I went on to say, "We do his math book, and his reading book, and we are reading a historical fiction book, and our Children's Bible, and I try to read a science picture book... I stay busy all day, but I still haven't gotten to our Latin workbook or our grammar books." My friend calmly replied, "It sounds like you need to get rid of some books."

Minimalism avoids the lure of "greener grass." I am acutely aware of the consumerism that exists in the homeschooling arena, and it is downright suffocating. We have all been tempted by that awesome resource that somebody recommended, or that was promoted at the last convention. Minimalist homeschooling is remembering that "want for nothing" is a far more useful cliché than "the next big thing" if you truly want to establish a mindset conducive to satisfaction, contentment, and ultimately, happiness. When you are deciding whether to use a resource, it is useful to apply a minimalist homeschooling filter:

1. Do I already have plenty in order to achieve our goals in that subject?

2. Does this resource suit our preferred schooling methods?

3. Is this the most valuable resource for achieving my goals in that subject? Am I willing to replace what I already have?

4. Will this resource keep my child moving forward in their body of knowledge, love for it, and/or use of it; progressing my child toward our educational goals and values?

5. Does this cover the specific things that I want my child to know, or that my child loves?

6. Can our schedule accommodate this resource?

7. Can I afford the space, time, and energetic cost of this resource?

Now you have identified how much time you have, your priorities, and your goals. It is time to choose the best resources for each subject. Minimalist homeschoolers choose the resources that help their homeschool reach its goals in the most effective and enjoyable manner within the specific amount of time that has been reserved. Guard your schedule against choosing resources that will demand more time than you have. Minimalist homeschoolers do the best things, not everything.

If you really do want to use a resource that will take more time than you have allocated, quickly go back to the beginning of your process and evaluate the resource against your values, priorities, and goals. Perhaps the curriculum has raised your awareness of values or goals that you previously missed. Resist the temptation to just add in extra. Can you make time elsewhere? Can you change your priorities this season? This process is flexible and each step that you take is offering valuable insight into your school.

I have provided a worksheet for this chapter to help direct your selection of resources. Even after you have made your final selection, you may want to keep this worksheet as a reference in case one of your selections does not work out as planned. Keeping a back-up list can offer a sense of security as you make the switch to a minimalist mindset, if you are afraid that you might not have enough. In minimalist homeschooling, achieving your goals is *enough*. Completing tasks with no distinct benefit beyond a sense of completion is extra; and *extra* means extra time, extra space, extra energy, and extra money. In this way, *extra* actually depletes our homes, our schools, and our families. Our homeschools and our families do not benefit from extra; we thrive with enough.

Regardless of what the specific goal is, minimalist homeschoolers deliberately work toward that goal, achieve it, stop, and move on. This idea of working toward a specific goal rather than toward completion may be new to many homeschoolers. Let me give you a couple of examples of how this looks logistically in a homeschool setting. If your goal is to ensure that your fourth grader masters long division, and you have purchased a workbook for long division in order to accomplish this goal, you will not do the entire workbook. Instead, work with your child to learn the long division process on the first few problems. Watch while they complete the next 5 problems themselves. Your time is probably up at this point, so you will continue the next day. Tomorrow, have your child do only the first 3 problems while you watch. If he or she is doing well, ask them to complete a certain number of problems alone in order for you to assess whether they have learned the process. Workbooks progress from easy to difficult, so ask your child to do the first 3 problems on a page and the last 5. Check to see how your child has done. If you find that they are struggling with any of the problems, work through the middle problems that you originally skipped together or while watching your child work. If your child got all 8 problems correct, move on to the next page tomorrow. You may even choose to skip a page or two at some point if your child has already breezed through that style of problems and the pages are just more of the same. Continue through the book in this way, assessing whether your child needs more practice at any point, or whether they can move forward in the book. At some point, you will notice that your child is getting all of the most difficult problems correct on their own. You have achieved your goal. Congratulate your child (and yourself), and decide on your next challenge! Perhaps you will save a few undone pages in your "math drills" folder so that they can practice again the next time math drills are part of your homeschool plan.

Be creative, and adjust this system for any lesson in any subject where your goal is mastery. Minimalist homeschoolers view pre-tests and review quizzes as tools to guide their lessons toward a goal. The principle is that you are led by your child's abilities, not by the design of a workbook, textbook, curriculum, or lesson plan. Resources, even whole curricula are used as tools, not a checklist. Minimalist homeschoolers are focused on their own specific and good goals, not the *shoulds* of the world.

The style of your lesson can reflect your goal. The previous example was for mastering a concept. However, if your goal is to practice a skill to improve proficiency, you may decide to finish the whole page, drill the whole set of flashcards (i.e. math facts), or work until the quality of their work begins to decline (i.e. handwriting). You might notice that your child has made no mistakes on their drills all week and decide to move on to a new workbook, skip some pages, or consider your goal achieved. If your goal is to have a fluent writer, you may choose for your child to write for a certain number of minutes each day; there are no other objectives, just let them write. Or read. Or create. In this case, a time limit is a perfectly worthy lesson plan. Do not forget to do a victory dance together with your child as you accomplish your high-value goals.

Through these imaginary situations, you can see how knowing your goal will focus your time and energy. Learning is more meaningful with deliberate and value-based schooling plans, determining when children can explore subjects that are meant to be explored, or drill subjects that are meant to be drilled. For example, if we drill history facts – when perhaps we have chosen that subject with the intention of influencing our children's sense of the world – we run the risk of losing their fascination and connection with the people, places, and intertwined events involved, and the actual goal will not be achieved. In this case, a resource that makes history relatable, or presents it as a story, would be a better suited to the goal than a set of fact cards.

"Should" is a dirty word in minimalist homeschooling. Keep your eye on the goal and prevent busywork done just for the sake of doing it. Minimalist homeschoolers do not think that a child *should* complete the whole workbook, or that they *should* do everything on a page: only whether we *want* our child to do tasks because they are valuable.

Also, minimalist homeschoolers remember that learning is more about *being* than doing or having. We are not hoarding facts to have. We are not doing schoolwork in order to check it off. We are *being* scholarly, we are *being* the best versions of ourselves. Our children are the best version of themselves if they can move at a pace that is appropriate for them; they are not necessarily reaching their potential when we finish every single problem in a workbook. Moving at a child's pace motivates them to do their best work every time. Children know when they have to complete a book and it does not require that all of the answers are correct. They know that it is busywork, and few children will be motivated to get them all correct. However, if they know that the point is to master a fact, they will work toward that goal, striving for correct answers every time so that they can accomplish their goal and move on.

Minimalist Homeschool Mindset Hack #31
Students reach their potential by moving at an appropriate pace, not by finishing everything.

There was a time when my husband and I felt like if we were distracted, at least our kids could do something educational. Once a child can read, there is no shortage of workbooks you can pile up, plus educational videos, apps, and books. So while I was busy with our baby, those are what the older children did, and a lot of it. But when I assessed what they had done against our goals, all that work had much less value. They were checking things off my list, not exploring the world as scholars, or experiencing the richness and challenge of new concepts.

Don't get me wrong, my children still have independent work, and we still watch videos, and use workbooks. The difference now is that we only use those things when they are truly valuable. All of our resources, including independent work, have been refined against our minimalist homeschooling filter to compile the most valuable resources, and therefore, are the most valuable use of our time. The flexibility comes in scheduling those items when it is best for children to work independently, based on each family's dynamic. Resources are not added simply because they keep children educationally occupied, but rather, because the best resources can be divided into those that require tutoring or supervision versus those that can be done independently. Make sure that your independent work is purposeful and not just a guilt-free way of occupying your children while you tend to (probably very worthwhile) other things.

Finally, it's time to make a lesson plan for your school! Since you have done all of the thoughtful preparations for your school, what was once a hair-pulling scenario is now actually the easiest step. The most important thing to remember as you place lessons into your calendar is that your schedule will dictate your lessons; lessons will no longer dictate your schedule.

Minimalist homeschoolers create lessons that can be completed within the amount of available time - they do not feel pressure to follow lessons just as someone else wrote them. You have done a tremendous amount of work identifying your values, how your time is spent, and the most valuable ways to spend your time. We have cast aside notions of *everybody else* and *should.* Making lesson plans is the time to make sure that we do not revert back to a mindset in which we defer to someone else to dictate our school. Instead, minimalist homeschoolers see resources as just that: resources. Our resources are not our instructions for our school. Minimalist homeschoolers use each resource in the way that best fits their school and their schedule, oftentimes in spite of different recommendations from the resource itself. Minimalist homeschoolers are not driven by the lesson times dictated by someone else, but rather, fit their resources into their schedule. This is one of the most important ways that you can stay in control of your time and energy.

Minimalist Homeschool Mindset Hack #32
Lessons are dictated by your time and values,
not by a resource.

In many cases, since your lessons are based on your child's pace, you will just write the name of the subject or the name of the resource in the appropriate place on your schedule. For example, you can write "math facts" or "handwriting practice," without listing a specific page. In the cases where you will be following lessons, or using all (or most of) a book, divide up your chosen resource into lessons that can be accomplished within the amount of time you have allocated for that subject. In this case, you can write things like "Narnia Ch 1," or "Science text 1.1 and 1.2." Place each lesson in the appropriate place on your schedule. If you are an experience-based schooler, place your most valuable experiences in the appropriate place on your school calendar. In this case, you may write "nature walk," "maker space," or "art museum" in the schooling block of your schedule. By the end, your schedule will be fitted with educational items that have been specifically curated for their value. In addition, your lessons are dictated by your available time. In this way, your resources are working for your school; you are not working for your curriculum.

There is a weekly lesson planning worksheet at the end of the chapter. It mirrors the worksheet you used to make a draft schedule, but it is rotated to provide more space for writing. Again, there are five sections to be labeled with days of the week. Each of those five sections has three compartments that can represent blocks of time, children, or lessons/independent work/group time. There are many ways to use this basic form to create a schedule that works for your family. Right now, use the form in the same way that you used it in the last chapter – identifying when subjects or activities will happen – but now add a specific task, or lesson. For example, what said "reading" in your draft schedule, will now list a specific book and chapter; it might say, "Trumpet of the Swan, Ch 1." Instead of "math" on this weekly lesson plan, you will specify exactly what task will be completed for math. Repeat this process, using your preliminary draft from the last chapter to guide and simplify your weekly plans.

Adding values and goals to schooling provides a sense of motivation. Assessing personal preferences makes schooling easier and more enjoyable. Carefully curating the best of the available resources and using them as tools saves time, energy, space, and money. Guarding our schedules for what is most important prevents overwhelm and makes more time. When families see value in their learning, and are not weighed down by an over-filled schedule or over-stuffed bookshelves, efficiency and productivity are naturally improved. In the end, minimalist homeschooling truly offers a more valuable education by doing less.

Know yourself: What do you know how
about how you teach?

Know your students: What do you know
about how your children learn?

LET'S **DO IT**

Minimalist
Homeschooling

RESOURCES & LESSONS

Child: Season:

Subject 1:   Resources (time req'd) $
Goals:

#2:
Goals:

#3:
Goals

#4
Goals:

#5:
Goals:

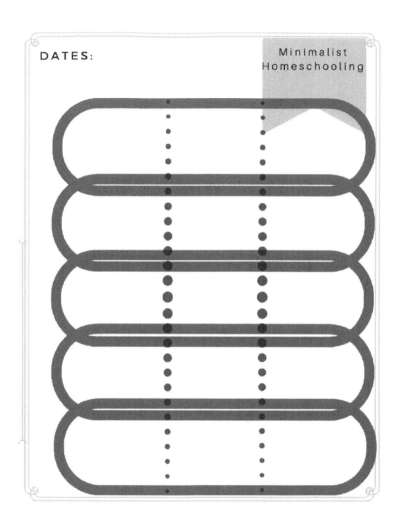

Chapter 6

SPACE & STORAGE SOLUTIONS

Do not store up for yourselves treasure on earth,
where moths and vermin destroy, and where thieves break
in and steal.
–Matthew 6:19 NIV

When you homeschool, your home is your school. If you want to simplify and declutter your homeschool, you must simplify and declutter your home. There are many benefits to simplifying your learning environment: time is saved when items are easy to find and clean-up, money is saved when fewer supplies and resources are purchased, and space is saved when you have only what you love and need. But perhaps most importantly, when we are striving to maintain focus on what is most valuable, eliminating visual and physical clutter can offer additional mental and spiritual clarity.

In this chapter, I will offer specific advice on how to begin simplifying your homeschool space and storage. In addition to elaborating on the minimalist homeschool mindset, there are specific action items that you can take to see immediate results. We are all busy with children and obligations (hopefully less so now that we have decluttered our calendars), so please do not try to accomplish everything in this chapter all at once. You do not need to complete everything in this chapter in order to call yourself a minimalist homeschooler, or to begin schooling minimally. I have to revisit this list regularly to continue my progress and maintain any minimalism I previously established. Taking action on even one item is an improvement and is moving you toward your goals.

I want to start by discussing how to store completed work. Decide on your filing system for completed items now. Children, if nothing else, are prolific in their work and creating. Minimalist homeschoolers decide exactly which items they will keep in advance and create criteria that schoolwork must meet in order to be saved. This is a good time to review state homeschooling requirements to make sure that you are cataloging items appropriately for your state. Next, choose a system of storage. Your storage system must:

1. Be easy to use and access.

2. Meet state homeschooling requirements.

3. Be limited by your predetermined criteria of which
    items to keep.

My favorite system for storing schoolwork is one box-bottom hanging folder per child per school year. Other people use one binder per child, sometimes filling the binder with sheet protectors in advance so that work can easily be slipped into its protector as the year progresses. A binder affords you the ability to separate items by subject more clearly. Also, a binder is a nicer presentation, if you feel that an auditor, you, or your student would like to flip through the accomplishments at a later date, or with any sort of frequency. Consider giving some of your child's precious schoolwork to a grandparent or godparent. An end-of-the-year portfolio of items that your child is most proud of can make a sweet gift and be rewarding for your child. I imagine that I will change my storage format when my students are older, in order to create a sort of portfolio. If you need inspiration, a quick web search will reveal all sorts of ideas for storing schoolwork. Your job is to find the system that appeals to your family and suits a minimalist homeschool. It is vitally important that your system is easy to use, conveniently located, and clearly defined in advance so that you can avoid piles of papers accumulating around your space.

Now that we have addressed storing and purging completed items, let's talk about the upcoming season of your homeschool. Minimalist homeschooling means your schooling resources include only those items which you have carefully curated for this school season. Do not include things that you have chosen for next year, or even next semester, in your current space. Do not include things that you hope you *might* get to. If you end up having extra time in a subject, trust that you can find something perfectly wonderful to fit into that slot when the time comes. Filling your resource area with things you will use later, or might use if you get the chance, creates physical and mental clutter.

We, as adults, are vulnerable to a sense of pressure and stress when confronted with a mountain of things to get done. Our poor children take on the same feelings when presented with a mountain of school books. There are so many options, yet they don't know where to start. It is easy for children to become over-stimulated in any environment – even an educational environment. We are well-intentioned; we believe that surrounding them with as many resources as possible will create a learning atmosphere, and therefore, we believe our children will love learning.

But what if our children scan over the whole bookshelf without noticing anything because it is crammed full, or are daunted by taking out one book due to the risk of creating an avalanche of books? Or what if, because the bookshelf has always been there with the same books, it has become familiar and uninteresting? Or what if our children dread school because they don't see a break, or an end, or an accomplished task, or a tangible goal – just a mountain of never-ending books and subjects? So, what if our best intentions to give our children the world, are actually smothering our children and pushing them away from what we actually want?

I think we can all agree that we want our children to sit down every once in a while, pick up a random book that looks interesting to them, and dive into it. We would like our child to notice a strategic game that exercises logic and spontaneously invite their brother to play with them after dinner. Is a huge, stagnant pile of books or games actually accomplishing that? In our house, the more options that were available, the less often my children made use of them. Minimalist homeschooling believes that a space is filled with things that are well-used and well-loved, and that extra is more harmful than beneficial.

Charlotte Mason and the author of Simplicity Parenting, Kim John Payne, have spent a great deal of time studying children and both argue that making decisions is exhausting for a child. Think about it: have you ever had a long day at the end of a long week, and your spouse asks you a benign question like, "What would you like to grill for dinner tomorrow?" and you can't even think about it? You plead, "Just make the decision please, I'm too tired to decide anything else right now." Your children feel the same way, although they are less likely to verbalize the frustration. Instead, they might say "I'm bored," or "I don't know what to do." More accurately, they're telling you, "Please simplify the decision for me."

Kids like open and clean spaces. Kids take pride in their space and their treasured belongings, too. They don't like chores any more than you do. They want their things displayed nicely, in a way that is easy to access and easy to clean up. If you are feeling overwhelmed, chances are that your children feel it, too, but may not be able to communicate it effectively. A child's sense of overwhelm may manifest as behavioral or mood issues. In our home, it had created a "have" and "get" and "take" mentality – one of ownership or lack thereof. When the focus was on who has what, kindness and helpfulness took a backseat and created an ugly atmosphere. Our home was no longer a place where we all coexisted peacefully, but rather, each child was trying to carve out his or her place, and his or her stuff. There was resentment about picking up other people's things: "But I didn't even play with that!"

Reducing the amount of stuff in our home changed the atmosphere of our home from a focus on what we *have* to what we *do*, and who we *are*. Similarly, changing the number of items in our homeschool changes the focus of our homeschool from what materials we have to what we are learning.

Now, I am not advocating a dogmatic rule for the number of books, games, or supplies each minimalist homeschooler should have. That would be hypocritical since *should* is externally imposed and minimalist homeschooling is designed around individual, purposeful action. Really, what I am saying is that minimalist homeschoolers constantly reassess their materials and do not passively allow things to accumulate. If your space feels full, cluttered, messy, difficult to use, stressful to clean, or excessive, then you have too much. If your space feels calm, content, well-used, well-organized, easy to use, easy to clean, and simple, then you have plenty.

Minimalist homeschoolers get in the habit of scanning their (sparse and tidy) shelves or bins to ensure that they still find each resource purposeful. Sections of the quick-guide in this chapter are second-nature to minimalist homeschoolers as they periodically assess their surroundings. Similarly, minimalist homeschoolers who do need additional materials will do the research to pick out exactly what they need to add – no more, and no less.

Minimalist homeschoolers instinctively switch out games and craft supplies when they notice that the ones that the children can access are not getting much attention. Since minimalist homeschoolers aim to have only items that are valuable, there are fewer of them, and so assessing the space and materials is itself a simple process.

Minimalist homeschoolers store and discard completed items throughout the year, and at the end of a year, they find a new home for any materials or resources that are no longer serving them. Consider keeping materials from your school year that you truly loved, and that you honestly believe your children would enjoy going back to again, and that they realistically will go back to again. Minimalist homeschoolers do not keep things because they *might* need them or use them again.

There are several options for finding a new home for your used items: online curriculum sales, local homeschool curriculum sales, Amazon, trash, friends, or non-profit organizations. Decide on your preferred method. Do it. Be honest with yourself about the amount of time that you are realistically going to spend adopting out these resources. If you might get $100 for your materials, but probably won't actually get around to selling them for a few months, I would recommend gifting them instead. Your space, time, and energy are more valuable than a stack of books taunting you from the corner of the room. Take the $100 charitable tax deduction by sending them to a nonprofit organization, bless others, and take pride that you have just appropriately valued your time. While you are at it, look critically at what you chose to keep from the last school year. Has your family truly enjoyed it over the past year? Some people want to hold onto items because the right person could really use it and so they wait for a chance to give a great gift. Trust that God will find the right home for your belongings – you do not have to control their destiny.

Minimalist homeschoolers prioritize space in the same way that they prioritize time – both are finite resources. Know what the function of each space is, and rather than trying to balance multiple purposes in one area, prioritize a space's function. If a space is used mostly for school, reading, and playing, then carefully assess whether everything stored in that space is used for those purposes. Then, group items within the room to set up zones – play zones, reading, zones, and school zones, for example. Although these zones are likely to overlap, having some separation will help with the use and clean-up of the space. This method provides a sense of purpose for the space that encourages clarity and focus. In contrast, a room filled with all sorts of things jumbled together can create an atmosphere of chaos, uncertainty, or overstimulation.

The kitchen is a space with an obvious use, but one that is most often multitasked inappropriately. Storing things that need to be fixed, or schoolwork, or business papers on kitchen counters is common. Minimalist homeschoolers think about where they actually tend to broken items, schoolwork, and business papers, and designate an aesthetically pleasing and appropriate place for them. While they are at it, minimalist homeschoolers are likely to designate an appropriate time on their schedule to fix broken items, file papers, and review schoolwork. Resist the urge to multitask your space any more than you multitask your time – it creates distraction.

Decide where you school. Again, minimalist homeschoolers are realistic, not idealistic. You may have designed a gorgeous schoolroom in the basement, but in reality, you are always working at the kitchen table. Be honest with yourself and do not fight your natural tendencies. It is easier to accept the reality of where you school, and create your space and storage around your family, than to try to change your family's habits and dynamics. Wherever and however you choose to school, store your resources accordingly.

Basically, to begin, you will need a place to store the items that you use every day and every week. This will be a space that is easy to access and near to your main schooling area. For families who school on-the-go, this may be a moveable crate. For families with a designated school room, there may be supplies at each student's desk. If you use different spaces for different subjects, then sometimes it is best to store your items accordingly. For example, store your art supplies near where you do art if that is a different space from where you learn other subjects. However, try not to scatter your items throughout the house – consolidating is a great way to simplify. There are many places to school in a home, and therefore, many ways to store your daily items. Whatever space you choose, use the quick-guide in this chapter to keep any space decluttered.

You will also need a second, separate space to store items that you use less frequently, or resources that are for another season. Store anything that you do not use more than once a month out of sight and seriously consider whether you really need it. This second space can be less accessible, but should still be easy to use and clean up. In the same way that minimalist homeschoolers allow their available time to dictate their activities, minimalist homeschoolers also allow their available space to dictate their resources. Avoid the temptation to fill your space beyond capacity. The concept is simple: If your resources cannot be easily retrieved and put away, then they are less likely to be retrieved or put away. This sounds obvious, but the reality is that so many messes, piles, and unused items are merely a result of inconvenient storage locations.

Minimalist Homeschool Mindset Hack #33
Items that cannot be easily retrieved and put away are less likely to be retrieved or put away.

Personally, I have daily supplies and resources in our dining room because that is where we do the majority of our at-home schooling. I also use a shelf in a hall closet where I keep materials that are age inappropriate, or cover different subjects than what we are currently studying. I have 4 kids and we work on a 3-year spiral through history and science, and so I have decided to keep several non-consumable materials. I also store hands-on learning materials and games in a closet so that a few things can come out at a time. It would be perfectly minimalist to donate or sell all age-inappropriate materials, and subjects for other seasons, regardless of how many children you have, trusting that God will provide exactly what you need in the season when you need it. You may choose whichever method you prefer. I highly recommend letting your available space and sanity be the deciding factor for how many items you keep. The quick-guide in this chapter will help you refine your spaces once you have identified them.

Let's talk about waste. A lot of people hold onto things because they don't want to "waste" a good thing. For example, half sheets of construction paper that were abandoned after the last project are collected and returned to the cabinet. For the next project, everyone wants a nice new sheet of construction paper. You will probably accumulate more scraps to add to your scrap pile after the next project. People do not want to just throw away all the perfectly good scraps – that would be a waste.

Either immediately design a project that uses scraps of paper, or throw those scraps away! And please, don't keep them because you *might* one day have a project that requires scraps of paper – I'm sure there will be more scraps available when that time comes. Those scraps are not getting used (i.e. they are being wasted) whether they are in the trashcan, or in your cabinet. The tragedy has already happened – only half of the page was used. Now, nobody wants that poor scrap. Whether it is in your cabinet or your trashcan, it is the same fate: nobody is excited to use that scrap. In reality, that scrap that you are afraid to "waste" by throwing it away, is now wasting your time whenever you organize it or search past it, and it is wasting space.

The same is true of the book that nobody wants to read. You can have the book on your shelf, or donate it, but either way, the book is not being read by your family.

Having an unread book on your shelf does not make it any less of a reject, or any less wasted. At least if the book goes to Goodwill, someone else may want to read it.

Apply this concept of waste now to every other school supply. The tragedy is not getting rid of what you do not use, even if you spent good money on it. The tragedy is that you spent money on it, and that the supply has been rejected or forgotten. There is no amount of storage or organization that will undo those two facts. Keeping it will not get your money back, for sure. The chance that you *might* one day like it, use it, or need it, is far less likely than the chances that you might not. Ever. It is a gamble that you are taking with your space, time, energy, and probably at least a little bit of your sanity. That's a pricey bet.

Minimalist Homeschool Mindset Hack #34
Items are wasted when they are
rejected or forgotten, not when they
are discarded or donated.

There are countless blogs, books, and Pinterest ideas for how to minimize, declutter, and simplify your home. There are entire books devoted to the subject. I fully encourage you to browse those resources to continue simplifying your space once you have finished this book.

In the meantime, I am going to offer a quick-guide to decluttering and simplifying your homeschool space. These are the methods I found to offer the most decluttering return for your time investment and that are especially useful in a homeschool. In general, the goal is to make clean-up and cleaning as easy as possible. If you notice any barrier that is deterring you from cleaning up, change it. There is a worksheet and a checklist at the end of this chapter to guide your space-simplifying mission.

<u>Space Simplifying Quick-Guide</u>

Reduce, reduce, reduce – Get rid of anything that is broken, unused, or unloved. If it is damaged, broken, or a bit of something, trash it. If you don't use it, get rid of it. If you love it, but you don't use it, question why you love it. Get rid of multiples, even if they are perfectly fine.

Ration school supplies – In the case of school supplies, it is common to have extras and sometimes it is prudent. However, I advise against having all supplies accessible all the time. Choose the best and most loved supplies for your active space. I store extra crayons, markers, paper, and notebooks separately in a secondary location. Keep your active space tidy and free from extras. Bring out new supplies as they are needed at the same time that you discard the used items that are no longer loved. It is fine to ask for gifts that are consumables like art supplies, but the trick is to keep some in reserve. A new kit will be fresh and exciting when your current supplies are worn-out and ready to be trashed. In contrast, when a new kit is added to a bunch of already great art supplies, it may not get much attention. Keep your daily area well-stocked with the best supplies. Just like books and curriculum, don't dilute your awesome supplies with materials that are just "meh."

Store things near their place of use – Nothing deters clean-up like having to lug things back to the basement, or to the other side of the house. Store items closest to where they are most often used.

Consolidate – Corral all similar items into one place. Avoid the temptation to have markers in each room and books scattered throughout the house. When designating space for specific tasks, also designate a space where task-specific items will be stored.

Use friendly storage solutions – Look at how your family is most likely to put things away. For example, bins are often more convenient than shelves or hooks. However, it is easier to find what you need from shelves. It is much easier to change your storage solution than to change your family's habits, so choose the storage solution that best matches your family's established behavior. You can expect more clean-up compliance when you work with your natural tendencies to hang, toss, or place items where they belong.

Use secondary storage – There is active storage, where things that you use daily are kept, and there is secondary storage for items used less often. Put the majority of your stuff in secondary storage: toys, games, out of season clothes, appliances, supplies, and books. Anything that is not used every week is a good candidate for secondary storage. Secondary storage can be a closet, higher shelves or cabinets, garage shelves, or a basement area. Make sure these items are well-organized and relatively easily accessible, but not cluttering your everyday space. Set a time limit to donate anything that you don't miss or use after it is stored.

Avoid obsessive sorting – Sorting things into too many categories can make clean-up tedious and intimidating. There are some exceptions to this rule – like art supplies –

but having a room filled with 15 bins that can be dumped, and then must be re-sorted upon clean-up, is a sure-fire way to sabotage clean-up.

Avoid too much variety – One way to avoid too many categories for sorting items, is to avoid having too many different items to begin with. Minimalist homeschoolers are experts at deciding which items have the most value and removing the less valuable extras. Extra items means extra space, time, energy, and money. Nobody can afford all that extra.

Clear surfaces – Surfaces that are completely (or almost completely) clear will automatically make a room seem tidy and will make a room easier to clean. Bare surfaces also encourage people to put things away.

Open floor space – Similar to bare surfaces, open floor spaces create a sense of visual calm and make a room seem uncluttered. Open spaces encourage creative play, motivate family members to keep it neat, and promote a sense of freedom.

The goldfish principle – It is said that goldfish will grow to the size allowed by their enclosure and so it is that messes will grow according to the number of available surfaces. The fewer pieces of furniture and surfaces you have, the fewer places there are for messes to accumulate. A surface tempts people to set things down.

Now or Never – Get in the habit of putting things away, instead of setting them down to put away later. It will take an extra 15-60 seconds to actually take that book upstairs to the closet, or it can sit on the bottom stair waiting for your next trip up indefinitely. Understand that if you do not do it now, it may never happen, or at least it probably won't happen very soon.

Point of interest – Consider having a point of interest to which your eye is drawn in each room. Often, this is a carefully selected wall display that is seen as soon as you enter the room. Then, make sure that the area around your point of interest is always tidy. This is one way to make a neat first impression.

Think vertical – Hang things on the walls instead of placing them on surfaces. This makes cleaning surfaces easier. You can hang photos, lamps, file folder holders, shelves, cute bags on hooks, and baskets on the wall. Be sure that they are the things that you truly love and need. Use this tip sparingly so that your walls do not look cluttered.

Multipurpose – To save on space and reduce clutter, use multipurpose furnishings. Use a storage chest as extra seating or a coffee table. Decorate with classic games or toys, beautiful books, globes, mirrors, or clocks. Think of things that you both use and love.

Use cabinets – Cubicles are all the rage, with canvas bins in every color, and they have their place in a home. However, opening and closing a door on a cabinet often makes it easier to see and get specific items. Closing doors is an easy way to ensure that a space looks tidy.

Use uniformity to your advantage – Contain small, or even large, items in sets of baskets and bins that all look the same. Uniformity creates a clean, less cluttered visual than random items, or various colors and containers.

Less is more – Do not fill spaces to capacity. Instead, only fill a shelf 2/3. Leaving contingency space makes it easier to get things and to put things away. Leaving room between things creates visual space, which is calming. It also means that if you do add an item to your collection, there will already be room for it, instead of immediately sending your storage into an overflowing state.

Trashcans – Put a trashcan in every room, especially your school room. If it is difficult to throw away trash, the trash is less likely to be thrown away. Period.

Accessible cleaning supplies – Just like trashcans, when cleaning supplies are handy, they are more likely to be used. Make them easy for your children to reach and use. Don't complicate cleaning supplies – a wet rag can handle most jobs. Consider an electric hand-held vacuum.

Schedule Clean-Up – Make time in your schedule for large purging and deep-cleaning sessions, as well as for daily tidying time. Hopefully we remedied your hectic schedule in Chapter 4, but when you are running straight from your lessons to a meal, and then frantically running to your evening activities, nothing gets put away. Messes accumulate. Check your schedule to make sure you can spare 5 minutes to put things away when you transition from one activity to another. Specific times when clean-up and chores are routinely expected helps simplify clean-up. Consider tidying every day before dinner, for example. You can have family clean-up time, or put chores on your child's daily school schedule. Personally, I have a goal to clean one room together as a family each day – each child is assigned a task in that room so it will only take a few minutes. You can do "power-put away" times when you set the timer for 10, 15, 20, or 30 minutes and race to throw away and put away as much as you can.

Delegate – Make tidying routines a habit. Delegate who will always put food away after a meal, wipe surfaces, load dishes, sweep, fold laundry, or any other number of household chores. Children can begin helping at a young age. Aim to give the members of your family standard chores that are non-negotiable and that happen at predictable times. Then, be persistent for 30 days to create a new habit. Repetition equals simplification.

Set time limits – If you are planning to fix something, repurpose something, do something, donate something, gift something, or sell something, set a reasonable time limit to get it done. If you do not get it done in a reasonable amount of time, clear it out of your home and life. The fact that you have not gotten to it means that it is not a high priority for you or your family. Your time has been filled with more pressing and important items. Those non-essential, low priority items have no place in an intentional home or life.

Clues from clutter – Look specifically at the items that are most likely to accumulate in your home and figure out why. Clutter is a symptom of some barrier to clean-up. Maybe those items do not have a proper home yet, or maybe their home is inconveniently located. Maybe your husband is more likely to put papers in a box than in a hanging folder. Maybe your son does not want to carry his toys back to his room when he only plays in the living room. Maybe you have been overly ambitious thinking you would sew the buttons back on all of those pants for the past five years. Look critically at your messes to identify the underlying cause and address the root problem.

Don't move the mess – When a mess accumulates, it is a sign that you have excess. Be sure to declutter (purge) your mess instead of re-organizing it or moving it to a different location. If your pile contains things you have been "meaning to get to," for months or years, then it is time to accept that it has not been worth your time, and is not likely to ever be worth your time, and then purge accordingly. If your mess has items that have not been missed in weeks, months or years, then it is probably time for them to leave your space. Resist the urge to organize rediscovered items that your family has neither missed nor needed.

Constantly purge – Minimalists declutter constantly. Decluttering is not a one-time event after which you leave it be. Rather, constantly throw away broken items, keep an ongoing bag for donations, and assess your items as you go through your daily activities. Get your donations and gifts out of the house on a regular basis so they do not accumulate either.

Set an example – Personally, the reason I used to be so frustrated with the messes in our home was because I felt like they were not my messes. It became easy to resent those I was living with as the source of the problem. In fact, I spent so much time tending to everyone else's messes that my own space (bedroom) never got the attention I wanted to give it. As a result, my room was the messiest room in the whole house. I was sacrificing my space to help everyone else. However, my children did not see sacrifice; they saw this as a sign of what was an acceptable use of space.

I encourage you to focus on your own space first for several reasons: First, to give yourself a sense of calm, peace, and accomplishment; having your own space serene is more rewarding for yourself than other people's space. This sense of peace will motivate you to tackle other spaces. Second, you can best control your own space. You have less control over spaces that others share. Third, it sets an example to your family of how you want spaces to look. It signals to them that it is worth your time investment. It also shows them how appealing a minimalist space is. When I clean-up one bedroom, my other children are likely to ask me to do their room next, because they prefer the clean and tidy feel.

Pace yourself – It is tempting to want it all done immediately. Changing habits, behaviors, and a mindset takes time. Practice patience with yourself and your family. Celebrate small victories and continue moving in the right direction. Minimalist homeschoolers value improvement over completion.

Minimalist Homeschool Mindset Hack #35
Become a space simplifying ninja –
use easy tricks to transform a space quickly.

Applying a meaningful focus to your education and your time is the best way to learn more while doing less, and a simple home is a vital component of your simple homeschool. Minimalist homeschooling is a liberating way to approach your home and your school in order to promote free time and free space. Instead of filling our lives with extra materials and extra subjects, we are creating more – more time, more energy, more space, and more value. A values-based and goal-driven education creates a simplified and intentional learning environment where students and teachers are motivated to succeed. Minimalist homeschooling is the best way to an excellent education without suffocating in options.

LET'S **DO IT**

SPACE & STORAGE

What are the criteria for saving
schoolwork?

How will I store our completed
schoolwork?

Where do we do the majority of our
schooling? Where will I store daily
(active) items?

Where will my secondary storage be?

What zones can I create to add purpose to
our space?

LET'S DO IT

SPACE & STORAGE

SPACE SIMPLIFYING NINJA CHECKLIST:

_ Discard broken, unused, and unloved items.
_ Remove "waste" from your space
_ Get rid of multiples
_ Trashcan
_ Cleaning supplies
_ Clear surfaces
_ User-friendly storage solutions
_ Items stored near their place of use
_ Ration school and art supplies
_ Consolidate similar items
_ Reduce variety; avoid excessive sorting
_ Move less popular items to secondary storage
_ Create open floor space
_ Move some items vertically
_ Create a point of interest
_ Allow time to clean & tidy
_ Keep spaces only 2/3 full
_ Be a clutter detective
_ Address your personal space
_ Multipurpose furnishings and decor

How will you reward yourself every time you simplify a space?

A NOTE FROM THE AUTHOR

I wrote this book for you in the hopes that you, too will find purpose in your homeschool and time in your days. My goal is to change your mindset in order to relieve the stress associated with a do-everything education in our have-everything society. If you have found this book helpful, please consider leaving a review so that this book can reach more homeschoolers who are looking for an easier and more meaningful way.

You can join me on Facebook at "Minimalist Homeschooling with Zara, PhD", or on Pinterest at "Zara, PhD." I regularly blog on the topic, create additional resources, and send encouraging newsletters from www.ZaraPhD.com, too.   You can always contact me by email at: hello@zaraphd.com. I'd love to see more you!

Wishing you all the simple things,

Zara Fagen, PhD

Made in the USA
Columbia, SC
15 March 2019

ABOUT THE AUTHOR

Often bristling at the formality of her title, Dr. Fagen prefers to be called Zara... or Mom. As a business owner and homeschooler, Zara advocates an intentional educational philosophy that eliminates the clutter, stress, and tedium associated with homeschooling, which she calls "Minimalist Homeschooling."

Zara keeps things as simple and as meaningful as possible in Indiana with her husband and four children. She is the President of her town's Parks and Recreation Board, and a governor-appointed member of Indiana's Midwifery Committee for homebirth midwives.

Zara earned her PhD in Neurobiology at the University of Chicago, and her research has been published in biomedical journals like the Journal of Neuroscience and Biochemical Pharmacology. She has a passion for reviewing the science in support (or not) of natural health options at scienceofnaturalhealth.com.

Zara blogs regularly about minimalist homeschooling at www.ZaraPhD.com, where you can find more resources, and link up.

Zara